Invisible
Illnesses and Disabilities

Rebuilding Your Life
By Learning To Live with
A Non-Terminal, Life-Altering
Situation

by Sharon E. Smith

Preface by F. Owen Black, M.D., F.A.C.S.
Director of Neurotology Research and
Senior Scientist, R.S. DOW-NSI

Printed in the USA by
Lifestyles Press/Hammer Publications
P.O. Box 493
Greensboro, NC 27429
1-888-742-2155

Cover design by Anthony Council

Dedicated to...

Bill, who has been a best friend, partner and soulmate, and whose love, support, patience and laughter always keep me going.

Mom, Dad and Tracy for their unconditional love and help in making the transitional points in my life smoother, and for their efforts to understand my situation and be supportive, no matter what circumstances arise.

John and Camille, for being the best friends anyone could possible have. For their taxi service, their help in the various hare-brained ideas I come up with, and their help in making this book a reality.

Bill's family and the friends I've met through Bill for their long-distance support (and occasional visits), letters and gifts, and for their concern and acceptance of me and support of Bill.

My extended family and friends for their well wishes, love, support and efforts to make my life easier.

Roberta, for being a long-time friend and supporter of me and Bill. She is truly part of our family.

Muffin, Taz, Buddy, Billy, Sweet Pea, Sam (and all of the other pets that have been in my life) for all of the love, companionship and fun that furry friends have provided me over the years.

All of the doctors and medical personnel whose skills and support have helped me get to this point in my life. I applaud your efforts to keep looking for, and learning about, ways to make disabilities easier to live with.

Acknowledgments

I would like to thank and acknowledge John Yoswick for being a terrific friend, and for reading, rereading, editing and re-editing the ideas that I have presented to him. His time, effort and encouragement have enabled me to share my story. I would not have been able to complete such an enormous task without him. I will always be grateful for his help.

Special thanks to Pacific University's physical therapy professors and staff (Daiva and Lori A., in particular) and to the physical therapy class of 1995 for their flexibility, concern and continued acceptance of me as a classmate.

I would like to recognize the "Jones" family (they know who they are) for their help the night of the accident. I will always be grateful for their willingness to come to our aid.

I also want to thank the relatives and friends who took the time to answer the survey I sent out. The questions were personal and difficult, and their honesty was appreciated.

For the time and feedback provided for the

finishing touches of this book, special thanks go to:
F. Owen Black, M.D.
Melissa Broomhall, M.D.
Bradley Coffey, O.D.
Camille Eber
John M. Epley, M.D.
Norma Epley
Robert J. Grimm, M.D.
Judi Grucella, P.T.
Beth Johnson
Bill Merritt
Ethelyn Pankratz
Gerald B. Rich, M.D.
Luigi Serio
Joan St. Jean, R.N.

Thanks to Beth Johnson for her creative ideas for the front cover of this book.

My sincerest thanks to Bob and Doreen Merritt for helping with the publication of this book.

Finally, thank you to the staff at Lifestyles Press for helping to make this book a reality.

Contents

F. Owen Black, M.D., F.A.C.S., P.C.

Balance and Hearing Center, NW; Otology-Neurotology

1225 NE 2nd Avenue, Suite 305
P.O. Box 3950, Portland, Oregon 97208-3950
Telephone: 503-233-6069; Facsimile: 503-233-8558

PREFACE
"Invisible Illnesses and Disabilities"
By Sharon Smith

"It is one thing for a man to understand a matter for himself and for his own use, and another thing to understand it and explain it for the use of others."
Peter Mer Latham (1789-1875)

Many patients are superior observers but have difficulty explaining their symptoms to others. Very few patients have the gift of articulating their problem in a way that is meaningful and instructive to others. Ms. Smith has accomplished these tasks with eloquence and sensitivity. It is difficult for one to imagine the enormity of such an undertaking considering the consequence of her accident.

Although I have seen Ms. Smith on numerous occasions and, I think, have an accurate medical history, many of the issues which she addresses that affect her life were not clearly understood. Consequently, I learned a great deal from Ms. Smith's effort. To her, I am deeply grateful. Her work has broadened my perspective of patients with head trauma.

The extraordinarily positive manner in which Ms. Smith approaches her life and its problems is exemplary. Her honesty and determination to overcome, to the best of her ability, the obstacles confronting her are not unlike many, indeed, most of the trauma patients I see. This book represents far more than a recitation of problems and a laundry list of "things to do about them." The experience with which Ms. Smith and her immediate support relationships deal effectively provides a sound basis on which to make recommendations to others. She offers practical suggestions that can be implemented by anyone who is unfortunate enough to experience a similar combination of injuries.

I recommend this book to patients, families of patients, and close associates of anyone who has had a head injury. *Invisible Illnesses and Disabilities* will enable those who care to positively influence individuals who struggle with the myriad of problems encountered after physical trauma.

F. Owen Black, M.D., F.A.C.S., P.C.

INTRODUCTION

This is a book about living life after being diagnosed with a permanent (though non-life-threatening) disabling condition. In my case, the problem is with my inner ear or, as the doctors usually refer to it, my vestibular system. However, if you suffer from a different kind of illness with a similar prognosis, this book is also for you. This is not a book about how to diagnose a problem, nor does it explain the vestibular system or other medical information in detail (that is available from other sources and briefly in Appendix 5 of this book). I am more concerned with sharing my story — my feelings and frustrations, and the steps that I have taken to learn to live and cope with a lifelong illness that most people can't see. I also provide some ideas and new ways to consider and handle situations that having such a condition creates.

I did not plan on writing a book. I was looking through bookstores for something that I could read that would help me understand and deal with a condition that is not a "terminal" illness. I was unable to find one, so using the daily notes that I had been keeping since the accident, I decided to write about my experiences in the hope that people who are in situations similar to mine will learn from, and perhaps enjoy, my story. I hope that you are able to relate to the problems, triumphs and emotions that I have gone through in the past several years, and will benefit from my observations.

Reading is a difficult task for me because of the concentration and eye coordination it requires. I have found that the brighter the paper is (the whiter or shinier), the harder it is for me to read. Matte-finish paper, greater space between letters and sentences, wider margins, and larger print all make reading easier for me. Others have told me they find this to be true for them as well. This book was designed with these things in mind.

MY OLD LIFE AND
THE ACCIDENT

- Some background information about myself
- The story of my accident
- My initial recovery
- A "relapse"
- Initial efforts to diagnose my condition
- An introduction to my illness/disability
- A battery of tests

It's too bad that people can't predict where and when life-altering situations will take place. If we could, perhaps we would be a lot better prepared when our "old life" ends and a "new" one begins. Even if we weren't able to change anything, a warning would allow us to start the long process of adjusting to the changes we would be dealing with in the near future. We could study whatever ailment, disability or situation we were about to face. We could inform our friends and family of our upcoming situation so that they too could understand what was coming and decide how they could deal with it and help us as well.

Unfortunately, we don't have that ability, so as most people would be, I was totally unprepared for what happened to me in the fall of 1991. I couldn't have known that I was about to begin an entirely new life — one full of questions, misunderstandings and pain, and yet one that, in its own way, is perhaps better and more fulfilling than the one I had known before.

I was twenty-two years old, was completing my fifth year of undergraduate work, and had just been accepted to a master's program in physical therapy at a university in Forest Grove, Oregon. Gaining acceptance into the program was no small accomplishment. Each year, thirty-two people were chosen out of approximately 450 applicants. I was to begin the program that fall, and was finishing the spring semester of undergraduate work.

I was not dating anyone at that time, and checking out some of my classmates, I singled out this cute guy I wanted to meet. I was taking a physics lab; he was teaching the same lab to a different group but would come in from time to time to talk with our instructor. We met a few times in the library, talked with each other at our apartments, and decided to go out on a date.

So on a chilly November evening, Bill and I met in the school library and went out for pizza. The restaurant we drove to was closed, so we drove around the back roads, took some photos, drove toward the beach, and talked until about four a.m. A few days later, on November 24, we decided to head out to the pizza place again. This time it was open. We ate pizza, had a beer, played several games of pool, and joked with each other. After enjoying that, we stopped to visit a friend, and then drove to a grocery store. After buying peanut butter cups, we decided to go out to try to get a photo of a rustic barn we had seen on our first trip.

I knew that I wanted Bill to meet my family, so while we were on our way to the barn, I was trying to muster the courage to ask him to join my family for Thanksgiving dinner.

It was slippery and wet out — a typical fall night in Oregon. As we drove along the back roads at about one a.m., trying to find the barn, we turned a corner, hit some gravel and started sliding off the road. I remember my heart sinking into my stomach as I realized what was about to happen. As we hit the telephone pole, I remember hearing the sound of the impact and breaking glass as I blacked out.

I regained consciousness sitting on the ground outside the car, holding my head in my hands. Bill was telling me to breathe. I looked at my bloody hands, and could feel a large gash in my head. We knew we had to get to a hospital and had no idea where we were. Bill had been driving my car, and from the look of the mangled heap left at the site of the accident, Bill knew it wouldn't be moving anywhere other than by tow truck to the junkyard. We walked to the only house we could see and

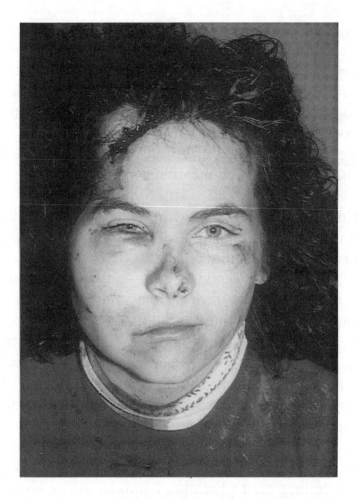

The auto accident left me badly disfigured

pounded on the door. It seemed like forever until someone opened it. It turned out that the people who lived there were afraid we weren't actually hurt and might rob them, something that had happened to some of their neighbors earlier in the month. But they called an ambulance once they realized that we needed help. (They actually called twice, the second time to warn the ambulance driver about the telephone pole that was now lying in the road.) I was trying to keep Bill from feeling bad; he was trying to keep me occupied and thinking about something other than my injuries. I remember him telling me that I was still pretty even though I was bleeding, and for some reason he asked me what the price of tea in China was. I remember telling him $14.95.

I was taken to the hospital and Bill remained behind to talk to the police. He was put through all of the police tests, asked how fast he was driving (only thirty-five mph, the speed limit), and was finally given a ride to his apartment with no citations. He changed his jacket, which was rather bloody, and got into his car to drive to the hospital to see me.

At about four a.m., a hospital nurse called my parents to inform them I had been in an accident and was okay. They were told that the nurse would call back to let them know how I was doing. My dad, who had answered the call, hung up thinking it was no big deal. He told my mom about the call and rolled over to go back to sleep. Mom was concerned, though, and persuaded my dad to go to see what had happened and how I was doing. I was relieved when I saw that they were with me. The nurse had not given them a very accurate description of my injuries, and once they saw that part of my head was open, my dad (having gone through a windshield in his younger days) called a plastic surgeon to sew me up.

The hospital took X-rays of the entire right side of my body and of my head. My face was so swollen that the neck brace was pressing into the side of my cheek. Finally, the surgeon arrived and determined that my neck was okay, so he began stitching me back together. It felt as though someone was scalping me while, at the same time, sewing my cut skin with no anesthetic. They couldn't give me any pain medication until they knew more about my head injury. Dad stayed to watch and hold my hand. I remember asking for Bill, and he was finally able to see me after the surgery. Dad told me that Bill had come over immediately after giving the police report. He stayed at the hospital the entire time I was there. I'm not sure who felt worse, Bill or I.

It was the first time he had ever met my family. I kept trying to tell him that it wasn't his fault, that it had just been an accident. He was driving at, or under, the speed limit, wasn't intoxicated, and wasn't doing anything erratic. It could have happened to anyone. Physically, he had a few bruised ribs, but he was feeling so guilty that there was nothing I could say to make him feel better. I heard later from the police that if he hadn't been paying as much attention as he was, the accident would have been worse.

Apparently, he saw that we were going to hit the

telephone pole directly on the front door where I was sitting, so he accelerated so that the direct hit was behind me. I also was told that I hit the windshield and the metal strip between the windows and the side window. If I had not been wearing my seatbelt I would have been killed.

For some reason I was sent home (under protest from me and my family) after being sewn up. I went home with my parents, took a few pain pills and fell asleep for about half an hour. I woke up thinking someone was killing me. I was shaking and sweating and white as a ghost, and I was in so much pain that I couldn't even make it back to the hospital without assistance. I thought that I was going to die. I remember asking my dad if I was dying. All I wanted, at that moment, was for the pain to stop. For the second time in twenty-four hours I got to ride in an ambulance. I was taken to a different hospital (by choice) where I was given a codeine antidote. I had been having an allergic reaction to the pain medication, and was having some kind of seizure.

I was there for three or four days. I was told by the nurses that Bill called about ten times that first day to see how I was doing. He came to visit me every day I was in the hospital. Bill didn't know if I would talk to him after everything that had happened, but we talked a lot after I was released. In fact, he has been with me almost every day since then. My family likes him a lot, and he is my soulmate and best friend.

The accident that changed my life

As I left the hospital and went to my parents' home to begin my recovery, I had no idea that the life I knew a few days before would no longer exist. I was just beginning a long journey of determining how and why my life had changed, and what I could do to either return to my old life or to begin a new one.

During my initial recovery, it was fairly obvious to anyone seeing me that I was hurt and in pain. My face was purple and green and swollen like a balloon (not many people can miss that). I also had trouble walking, standing, reading and breathing. For a few months I couldn't see well, the pressure in my head was enormous, the headaches wouldn't go away, and some bright lights and smells bothered me.

Day by day, the swelling went down, and my physical ailments disappeared. I was able to start school in the fall, but I soon started to experience problems. It was harder to remember lists of things. I was getting migraine headaches. I had a hard time integrating information from my classes. Sometimes I could not remember what I had for breakfast or what I had done the day before. I also had been fairly fluent in Spanish before the accident, and I could no longer hold a conversation in Spanish or think of words that I had once used easily. About two months into the master's program, I woke up one morning and felt as though I had regressed to the time shortly after the accident. I could barely stand or walk, and I felt sick. I assumed I would feel better soon, so I fumbled my way through two days of school. I couldn't tell you a word of what anyone said during that time.

Finally I was about ready to collapse and was taken to the hospital for tests. They ran an EEG, EKG, CT and all those other lettered tests and found "nothing different." Little did I know that these tests would go on for about three years. Because I still had short-term memory problems and trouble with my balance, I had to drop to half-time in school (an unusual thing to do, but the school was extremely accommodating). I studied nearly every waking moment of those months and barely passed my courses. I would try to memorize something on a page, then would look at a new page and all the previous information would be gone. After several months, I had to drop out of school. I could barely hold myself up, let alone a physical therapy patient. I was also spending so much time with different doctors and being tested that I had little time left for much else.

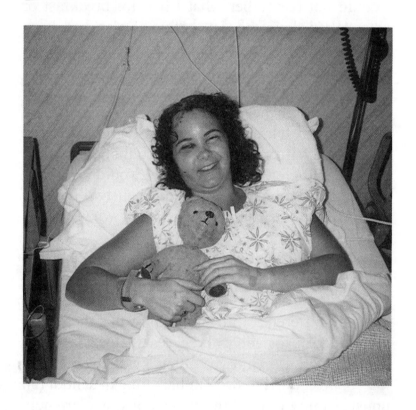

Recovering with bear at my side

After analyzing several of the tests that had been run, my doctor determined that I had vestibular (inner ear) damage. I set out to learn more about it and to find out if "it" could be repaired. This damage was what was causing my balance, memory and other problems. The balance mechanism in my ears was not working, causing me to feel continually dizzy and sick.

When a person's inner ear is not working optimally, he/she may feel sick or queasy, the way some people do when riding in a car or on a carnival ride. The best description I can give for the day-to-day sickness and dizzy feeling that people with inner ear problems experience is that it is similar to having a really bad hangover (without the enjoyment of the party the night before). It can also be likened to having a horrible flu — when the room is spinning and it is difficult to walk to the bathroom without your knees giving out on you. The headaches, dizziness and nausea are a regular feeling for people such as I.

I basically have lost the ability to know where I am in relation to the ground or anything else without being able to see. I can't balance with my eyes closed — or even sometimes when they are open. Everyone relies on three things for balance and to know where they are in "space" — their sight, their vestibular system, and proprioception, the information our bodies receive from joints about where our arms and legs are in space. I can only rely on my sight and proprioception. If it is dark or my visual field is blocked or overloaded, I have only touch and proprioception information to help me. I imagine that astronauts experience this lost, sick and dizzy feeling in micro-gravity, before their bodies acclimate.

If, for any reason, you would like to try to make yourself feel this way, close your eyes and have someone spin you around about twenty times. Then have them guide you to a piece of foam rubber. Stand on the foam and, without opening your eyes, try to balance and walk.

Or make yourself watch that long, poorly-shot home video of your uncle's adventure around the world (the one that would have been pretty interesting if the camera had not been continually bobbing and moving around, thus making everyone watching it "seasick").

Another technique would be attempting to walk in a straight line with your eyes closed right after spinning yourself around (the way you probably did when you were a kid) or after going on dizzying carnival rides. During those initial moments after you actually stop moving, your body feels as if it is still in motion. That is the way I feel many days. I sometimes refer to the way I feel as if I were walking on stilts or moving in slow motion (I also termed this "reverse warp speed," for you "Star Trek" fans.) When I move my head, there is a time lag before my eyes catch up with whatever I am doing. Crowded areas, large groups of people and even certain noises, such as certain voices or a certain pitch or volume, can cause these symptoms to increase.

Several months after the accident, I described all of these feelings to an ear specialist and was sent to a special laboratory that is designed to track vestibular conditions. The tests there are not fun. One of them involves trying to balance on a moving platform while having your body and head enclosed in a box speckled with dots inside it to distract the visual system. The box is also moving, adding even more stimuli. Fortunately, one is secured with a parachute harness attached to the ceiling during this test, so that if he/she falls, he/she doesn't knock him/herself out. While doing this test, one is also hooked up to electrodes that track his/her movements via computer.

Another test involves sitting in a specially-designed chair with the electrodes on and hooked up to a computer. The room is pitch black. The only thing one can see is a red electronic dot on one of the walls. The chair initially is positioned so that one is staring directly ahead at the red dot. Then the red dot disappears and the chair starts to spin or rock from side to side following a specific computerized program. While the chair is still moving, one is asked to answer a series of questions to keep him/her alert and from concentrating on his/her eye movements. The chair moves for several minutes for each programmed pattern, and then stops before the next movement begins. After each time the chair stops, one must look at the red dot again (it appears after the chair stops moving), and the computer records eye and chair movements and compares them.

A similar and sometimes more nauseating series of tests involves watching a series of vertical squiggly lines on the walls of the darkened room while seated in the moving chair. About three seconds into this four-minute test, my heart rate shot sky high and I started sweating like crazy. During these series of tests, one is lucky if he/she doesn't throw up.

The prize winner for me, however, was a test in which they insert a little balloon-like thing in one's ear. The balloon is gradually filled with cold or hot water. The drastic temperature change in one's inner ear can cause her to feel that she is spinning out of control (which is what they want, so they can record stimulated eye movements). This "lovely" test is generally done four times, twice with hot water and twice with cold.

There are many other similar tests that are designed to pin-point vestibular problems. Although each test is different, all are designed to track eye and body movements, and are supposed to give the doctors more information about the patient's particular ailments. The initial tests didn't help the doctors much in my case, however, and I was "lucky" enough to have to do most of the tests twice. The second day of testing didn't give us much more information than we already had. I continued to see the ear specialist and got to do fun things such as leaning forward in a chair and then quickly hurling backward to lie down, while everyone watched to see what my eyes were doing. They did tests with sound and pressure in my ears, trying to determine if both ears were affected or just one. The consensus was that both ears were probably involved, but that my right ear was causing me more trouble.

I also went through a procedure that involves puncturing the ear drum. It was done twice. (In retrospect, I think I am a total idiot for letting myself go through that a second time, but as they say, "Hindsight is 20/20.") The idea behind this procedure is that, by equalizing the pressure in the ear, some of the dizziness and balance problems would disappear. What actually occurred for me was the opposite of what was intended. I was more dizzy and nauseated than ever. This procedure was even worse than the other tests because the dizziness lasted for weeks, instead of a few days.

About two years into this routine of up to seven medical appointments a week, it was determined that I had small amounts of spinal fluid leaking in my ears. My doctor explained that, because of the accident, the membranes that would normally separate my inner ear from my middle ear had holes in them which were leaking inner-ear fluid (perilymph). The doctors refer to these holes as fistulas. My ear doctor would try surgery to patch the leaks.

Off I went to the land of anesthesia and surgery. This is a weird place. I remember talking to the nurses and doctors and being given some sort of sedative. The next thing I was aware of was that my throat was hurting, the room was spinning, and I was throwing up. This was especially odd for me because I am the type that will hold it down if possible. My motto is usually: "At all costs, don't lose your lunch!" But I couldn't help it.

It was supposed to be a quick out-patient procedure, but I watched hospital roommate after hospital roommate leave while I was still there vomiting. I was finally released from the "23-hour unit" about 22 1/2 hours after I got there, still feeling no better than when I woke up. I was told to sleep in an upright position for the next three or four days (I slept in a chair), and never bend over, pick up anything heavy, or do any kind of activity that causes exertion. The hope was that, after my body got over the initial shock of surgery, I would feel relief. In my case, that didn't happen.

By this time, my doctor was really getting frustrated and confused. He had tried his best to find and treat my ailment, but he was unsuccessful and didn't know what to do next. In a wise decision, he referred me to another specialist for a fresh start and a new outlook.

THE MIDDLE OF THE ROAD

- Referrals to new experts
- My recovery continues
- Complications with my diagnosis
- A trip to the "sleep lab"

The man I was referred to was a neurologist specializing in vestibular problems. He spent about three hours in our initial visit just asking questions and taking notes. I felt comfortable with him immediately. He would listen to what I had to say. He always involved me in decisions, acknowledged my understanding of human anatomy because of my physical therapy work, and explained everything in a very laid-back and straight-forward manner.

When I went to see him for the second time, I told him I had noticed several new symptoms. I had a severe pain, mostly behind my left eye, that got worse with eye movement. I noticed that the right side of my forehead had a large bump on it, where some of my headaches were located, and that I had been extremely fatigued (more so than normal). I had ended my period recently, and had noticed that usually around that time every month my symptoms were worse, possibly due to the hormonal changes that occur during a woman's cycle. I had also noticed that the weather seemed to affect how I was feeling. The doctor said that abnormal or damaged ears may be sensitive to barometric pressure, so weather could affect my symptoms.

Another problem was that my pupils were rapidly fluctuating between dilation and constriction. I noticed this happening more at night or after I had done something strenuous. Sometimes the pupil changes occurred without a reason. I later found out that it was due to the spinal fluid leaking, some brain-stem damage I had sustained, a vision-focusing problem and overexertion. My mom pointed out that I had a facial droop that changed hourly and daily. She noticed this because my smile looked different in certain photos of me. This, we think, was also related to how much activity I had engaged in during the day.

When I saw an ophthalmologist about the pain in my eye, he determined that the impact of the crash had fractured part of the bone behind my eye, leaving a small crack. When I moved my eye, it would often catch on the crack, causing the pain. I also had some bleeding in the eye itself, but both problems dissipated over time and no treatment was necessary.

Having my body go through all of these changes left me feeling extremely irritable. I was tired of talking to my family and to people who thought they knew what I was going through. In reality, they had little or no idea. I suppose my illness was a hard thing to describe, but I was getting very tired of explaining it and of listening to everyone's ideas of what I should and shouldn't do. At one point, someone suggested that I should have dinner on the table daily and always have the house cleaned because I had nothing better to do. My parents had said similar things from time to time, perhaps forgetting that I was at home because I wasn't well. I think sometimes people thought I was being lazy and believed I had more energy than I actually did. What they did not see or realize was that sometimes just getting up and getting dressed in the morning exhausted me.

During this time, Bill gradually spent more and more time with me, spending the nights in my parents' spare room and driving back to school during the day. During the summertime he moved into the spare room, although he still had his own apartment in Forest Grove. It was very comforting to have Bill around, but it was also an awkward time for everyone.

Being an adult and moving back in with my parents was difficult, but Bill's adjustment was even greater; that is, living with a family he was gradually getting to know, and living just down the hall from me, his girlfriend.

Somehow we managed to make it through those

days, though, and despite all of the discomfort and difficulties, Bill and I were able to move out of my parents' house (more than three years after the accident) and into an apartment of our own about ten blocks away. That was a very good move for everyone. My parents needed their space, and we needed ours, and, in particular, I needed to regain some measure of independence. The transition was a bit difficult, but we have almost everything we need on one floor (washer/dryer, dishwasher, etc.), and Bill and I can do the housework a little at a time.

This move was made possible, in part, because the neurologist referred me to one of the country's leading specialists in vestibular disorders, and they worked together to try to diagnose my condition. This specialist was the one who observed another complication in my medical situation. After asking me if I was sleeping well (I hadn't been), he sent me to a specialist in sleep disorders.

Time for more fun tests in the hospital sleep lab. I had electrodes hooked up on my face, arms and legs with some kind of cement (after having my skin scrubbed raw with liquid sandpaper so that the electrodes would stick). A microphone was taped to my lips and I was told to try to "relax and get a good night's sleep." While sleeping, one's sleep cycles are monitored and any snoring, talking, or breathing difficulties are noted. We learned that I do stop breathing several times during the night, a condition called sleep apnea. I also was getting very little

REM sleep, the sleep in which one dreams, and my legs twitch a lot while I am asleep (this is common among those with vestibular problems). These interruptions in my sleep were contributing to my fatigue and, possibly, affecting my vestibular condition.

With this information, I went back to the inner-ear specialist, who determined that the increased head pressure associated with my sleep apnea was keeping the holes in my ear membranes open, allowing the perilymph fluid to continue to leak. This was causing part of my headachy feeling, the pupil changes and the feeling of having a hangover. He hoped that treating my sleep apnea would allow the holes to heal. At night, I was hooked up to a machine that pushed air into my system, to try to keep my airway from collapsing. After trying several different versions of this machine (which really made me feel old and unattractive), they determined that the machines were actually making the ear problems worse. I continued to be the medical exception to almost every rule. Aside from sleeping with my head and chest elevated (which decreased the apnea episodes somewhat by decreasing the force of gravity on my airway) and taking some medications that would keep my airway from collapsing and my legs from twitching excessively, I was not a candidate for any other type of treatment or surgery. This meant that there was nothing that could be done about the periodic reopening of my perilymph fistulas.

It was then that I was given a long list of things that would likely make my condition worse, and was told to follow a diet regulating sugars and salt (so that the fluid pockets built up in my ears wouldn't swell or shrink drastically, causing more dizziness). I also was told to regulate my caloric and fat intake because I was not allowed to do any type of regular exercise. I was then sent on my not-so-merry way with the prognosis of having to live with what I had. I now had to accept the fact that I was not going to be "healed" and that my life was going to be a lot different than the one I had planned.

BEGINNING MY NEW LIFE

- New restrictions to deal with
- Breaking points
- New goals and activities

I now have many restrictions, but I have learned how to deal with a lot of these inconveniences, and have persisted in my desire to do things and to keep in contact with the medical experts. I am not able to fly in an airplane, swim or be in water, exercise, bend over, or push, pull or lift anything over five pounds. I have to be careful not to "blow my nose" or stifle sneezes, and I am on medication to keep constipation from being a problem. I can no longer go on carnival rides (boo!), and am not supposed to be jumping out of airplanes or bungee jumping (not a problem there). I had to quit playing the saxophone (that was a hard one) because I am not to do any activity that will increase pressure inside my head, abdomen or chest.

I am also supposed to watch my sugar, salt, caffeine, aspirin and alcohol intake, always sleep with my head and chest elevated, and call the doctor immediately if I feel a cold or flu coming on, because I am susceptible to meningitis and other viruses, with my inner ears being open to the outside world due to the fistulas. I am not able to work or go to school because of the daily and, sometimes, hourly changes in my stamina and general health. I've even found that crying, sneezing, coughing, or laughing hard for any length of time can cause my symptoms to become worse. (I'm not sure it's possible to stop any of these normal body functions, and it is definitely not desirable to stop laughing, so I'm not going to try or advise anyone else to do so either!)

A difficult thing for me to deal with in trying to become comfortable with my new life is the fact that I get grumpy and irritated very easily, especially if it has been a long day and I am tired. I can recognize the fact that I am getting grumpy and then I get mad at myself and get even grumpier. I am surprised at the speed with which this can happen. Most of the time it comes on very suddenly. It's usually when I am tired or my "circuits" have been blown (the feeling that I get when I am being overloaded with stimuli, information or noise). I feel as if I am a circuit board, and each noise, movement or sensory input is like another appliance being plugged in. Pretty soon there is too much going on and the circuits start to blow out. That is my brain. Click, click, click, and there is no more juice to fuel the appliances. This is when panic mode can set in, or I get very testy.

Although I realize that this happens to me, by the time I am in the situation it is usually too late to do anything except go somewhere quiet to rest. This can be hard on the people around me. One minute I am doing okay, and the next I am just about to go nuts and can easily blow up at them. Sometimes just about anything can make me cry. At these times I am usually unable to make decisions without "brain overload," and I am not able to function very well. I have worked hard at keeping control, but I still have not perfected being able to tell in advance when it is happening, so it still does. Usually by the time I can tell, I am past the point of no return. The people I am around the most can usually recognize when this has happened, and are pretty good at helping me get somewhere where there is little going on.

A variety of things can trigger this "emotional overloading." If I am asked too many questions at a time, it can happen. If there is more than one conversation going on in a room or if I am in a crowded place and I am unable to focus on one thing to stabilize myself, it can happen. Even if I don't go anywhere, sometimes being in the same place for too long gets to be frustrating, and my frustration overloads my system.

Part of me knows that I can do little to prevent these episodes, but the other part is constantly feeling bad when it has taken place. I feel dumb and guilty for having been unable to calmly get myself through it, and that I won't immediately feel better by sitting down to rest (sometimes it takes days).

I give Bill, my friends, and my family a lot of credit for being able to accept these episodes and still be able to endure me. Sometimes I am hardest on myself and load myself up with tremendous guilt and regret (I am working on that, too) that my family and friends don't see. But, other times, I can't help letting all of the worries and irritation out, and it usually lands on one of them. Bill and I do pretty well most of the time dealing with this stuff, but when he works all day and comes home tired, I have been home all day and am sick of seeing the same walls, so it is hard to compromise at times. He wants and needs to rest, and I feel that I need to get out of the house.

I am fortunate in that some of my friends and most of my family live nearby and are considerate about taking me places, but I still end up spending an extraordinary amount of time in the same place. For some reason it is not as bad in the fall and winter because, in Portland, it is often raining and miserable-looking outside. On these days I can usually be content with staying inside and baking or working on a craft or hobby. It is much more difficult in the spring and summer, however. There is a part of my brain that starts to act up during these days saying to me, "I WANT TO BE OUTSIDE DOING SOMETHING!" Unfortunately, I can't do the things I used to do outside such as exercising, walking or sunbathing (I don't want skin cancer, too), so I have difficulty being content inside during the nice weather days.

The funny thing is that when I am outside for a barbecue or other events, I am usually not very comfortable either. The bright light and heat bother me, and I have this phobia of bees (I think I got stung too many times as a kid). So between the bees (which I see as the size of large dinner rolls, no matter how small they are) and the brightness, I am usually not any happier out there. Sometimes a nice shady spot is just the right thing, but the shady spots near our apartment are in the parking lot, so it's not too often that I want to sit out there. I really miss being able to take walks outside. That used to be one of my favorite things to do, especially in the fall when it is cool and crisp and the leaves are colorful. I haven't found anything to replace that experience.

Something that has helped me stay somewhat active has been my experience with a vestibular physical therapist. I started doing some eye and balance exercises with a physical therapist who was recommended to me by my ear specialist. My therapist and I also worked on keeping some of my muscles toned by doing some low-intensity walking on a treadmill. We started at one minute of walking and worked up to a daily maximum of ten minutes at a time at the speed of 1.1 mph on the treadmill. We were careful about monitoring my pulse so that I did not reach anywhere near a "normal" person's training heart rate (otherwise I would be exerting too much pressure and the ear problems would get worse). My therapist was great and I liked her a lot. She was relaxed and patient and, although we did not expect a miracle, we were trying to re-teach my nervous system how to do a few things more efficiently. It was, and still is, surprisingly difficult work. I find I

It takes almost a week to complete one of my cakes. I make the icing one day, color it the next, and then make the cake the following day. Then it takes a few days to decorate it.

am usually exhausted after doing exercises a "normal" functioning person would breeze through, but each therapy session has helped me feel more alive and mentally healthy.

I have learned that I can do a few things I really want to do by resting in advance (although I still know I may feel exhausted in the days that follow). My weekly cake decorating class was a good example. I was usually wiped out after it, but it gave me something to look forward to, and I could prepare during the week for the next class. I still decorate cakes and people ask me why I don't "go into business" when they see my cakes. They also don't realize that it takes me about a week to complete one. I make the icing one day, color it the next day, and then make the cake the following day. Then it takes a few days to decorate it. Nevertheless, I enjoy applying my limited energies toward something I enjoy and in which my competence is growing.

GRIEVING

- *Coming to terms with your losses*
- *Help from family and friends*
- *Going back to the scene of the accident*
- *Some reflections about the night of the accident*
- *One of my most difficult days*

A disabling condition, whether it is apparent to others or not, leads to many losses: the loss of mobility, the loss of career options, the loss of individuality and independence, and the deprivation of many other things. All of these life changes require grieving, and you must allow yourself to do that in order to move on.

How do you go about grieving for all of your losses? Well, time helps, but not many people want to hear that. Talk about your feelings with someone you trust. Try to get out of the house, even if it is to go to the store. Find new hobbies and things to keep yourself occupied so that you don't think about your situation as much. When none of these ideas works, sometimes you just have to get through the day and let yourself feel bad — not too long, of course, just for awhile.

After leaving school and moving back in with my parents, I wanted to try to find the people that had helped us the night of the accident to thank them. I had not seen them since that night. I also felt that going back would help me to begin my healing process. Bill and I took some gifts as a thank you on Christmas Eve, a month after the accident, but they were not home. We stayed for awhile to look at the area where we had slid off the road. (I wanted to see if an earring I had lost that night was still around — it wasn't.) There were still peanut butter cups in the grass (I remember one had a fat slug on it) and the telephone pole had not been replaced. (We received a bill for about $800 for that thing! Fortunately, the insurance I had through my parents' policy paid for everything.) While we were there, someone from the neighborhood asked us if we were the ones that had hit the telephone pole. We told him we were, and he shook his head saying ours had been the fifth or sixth car that had hit that same pole that year.

On my birthday five months later, I stopped by the scene again to try to say thank you in person. Those who had helped me were grateful that I stopped. They had tried to find me through the school to see how I was doing, but were unsuccessful. I feel very fortunate that they were there to help. Every year at Christmas, I send them a card reminding them, as well as myself, of my gratitude. They have reciprocated the card exchange, and I feel good about that.

Going back to the scene of the accident was strange. Everything looked different from the way I had remembered it. The house wasn't miles away as I thought — it was just across the street — and there wasn't a large field anywhere in sight as I had "remembered." In fact, there were houses just about everywhere we looked; the night of the accident, I remember being able to see only one. The walkway of the house seemed like the longest one on the planet that night, and in reality, it was fairly short. It was difficult to revisit the scene, but, at the same time, I felt compelled to do so, as if part of me needed to see where my life changed in order to deal with what had happened to me since then.

The loss of my ability to drive was, and is still, one of the hardest things for me to accept. It means giving up precious freedom, individuality, and my ability to be spontaneous and self-reliant. Not being able to drive requires always relying on someone else unless you can take the bus, are able to walk, or can afford to spend money on cab fare. The problem with the bus for me is that I have to exert myself to get to the bus stop. Then if I get somewhere and feel fatigued, how do I get home? How do I buy something and take it home if it weighs more than five pounds? And I just don't feel safe. I don't even feel safe walking down a flat street alone because I am unstable and tire easily — I am a prospective victim of criminals. I would like to take a self-defense or karate class, but with my unstable balance, coordination and stamina, I don't think that will be happening any time soon.

Having to rely on other people to get me places is frustrating. I can no longer go somewhere when I feel like it just to get away, or go to the mall to go shopping by myself. This is particularly inconvenient when trying to buy a gift for someone, or do something to surprise people. Almost every time I go somewhere, I am with someone else, and when I am alone, I am usually at home looking at the same walls day in and day out.

I have found several ways to maintain a little independence. One solution is to have someone drop you off somewhere, and arrange to have them pick you up in a few hours. Taking a taxi would work, but it can be rather expensive. The bus alternative works for some people, although it's hard to do anything spontaneously. Also, some cities have door-to-door transportation for those who qualify for it, so that may be an option as well. The best way to deal with the transportation situation is to just learn to accept that you have to do things differently.

Grieving is a good thing to do, but it is also important to focus on what you have and what you are able to do. My dad told me one day that I should take a lesson from Julio Iglesias. At one point in his life, Julio was a great soccer player, but he was injured and was never able to play competitively again. Instead of living in grief and focusing on all that he had lost, Julio learned to play the guitar and sing. Those were things that made him happy and that he enjoyed. He went on, as the commercials say, to sell more records than even Elvis and The Beatles! Just as one door closes, others — perhaps greater opportunities — will appear. It's up to you to look for those doors and open them. (My dad suggested that, if some day I am well enough to open a bakery, I should include "Julio" in the name of my store.)

One of the things that made my grieving easier was that Bill formerly worked for himself and had a flexible schedule. He was able to take time off in order to help me get somewhere, or just to be with me so we could talk. He has also always been very considerate and conscientious about trying to take me places for a change of scenery. My family has also been very close by, and they all have been helpful in being available during the difficult moments that have come and gone.

One of the most difficult days for me since the accident was the day that the class I started my physical therapy master's program with was graduated. I had kept in contact with several of my classmates and professors after dropping out of the program, and was invited to their graduation brunch. I was very happy for them, but the reality of my situation had never affected me as deeply as it did that day. I was not going to be a physical therapist. I was not going to get the job I had dreamed of since college. I was not going to earn a good living. I was nowhere near where I had expected to be four years earlier. Not even close. I have always been someone who had long-term goals, and would work on achieving those goals until they were achieved. I didn't have even one goal then.

This outcome was difficult for Bill too, because when he and I met, my plans were to go through school, get my master's degree, and then work at something I loved (making a good living too, I might add). Now he is the one who has to work, and he hadn't really decided what it was that he wanted to be doing. I knew what I wanted to do, and I didn't get to do it. Facing that reality is tough — even when you're facing it with someone you love.

Although that day was particularly difficult for me, it was also an important turning point in my life. It became obvious to me that day that all of the things I had gone through and endured would be with me forever. If I wanted to live a happy and fulfilling life, I would have to accept things as they were, and begin to look toward more positive alternatives in order to enjoy living my new life.

DIFFICULT ADJUSTMENTS: HOW AND WHERE TO START

- Some personal adjustments
-Dealing with suggestions and ideas from skeptics and "know-it-all's"
- Intellectual changes, emotional challenges and issues of self-esteem
- Ways to conserve energy and adjust to your new situation

Having vestibular problems makes almost every experience different for me than it used to be. Riding in the car is a good example. I was never one to be car sick or queasy before the accident, but now I certainly understand the feeling. Riding in the car is my basic mode of transportation, although often I am not comfortable with it. I get sick from the movement of the vehicle and not being able to tell where I am. Being in the front seat is better than in the back. Driving during the day is better than at night, and driving in fog, heavy rain, hail, snow or anything that makes seeing out the window impossible is REALLY bad. U-turns, zipping in and out of traffic and "brake riders" can be nauseating.

Sometimes you just have to put up with whoever is driving since they are doing you a favor by getting you where you want to go, but sometimes it helps to tell people the things that are bothersome, and you hope they will adjust a little without compromising safety. For some reason, for example, a three-point turn is easier for me to handle than a U-turn. And either a fast U-turn, or an extremely slow U-turn, is worse than one done at moderate speed. It's sometimes hard to tell and remind people about these sorts of things, and for them to remember. But remember that they probably want you to be comfortable and would want to know how they can help.

Another major adjustments for me was that during my initial recovery and scores of appointments with doctors, I required a lot of sleep (fifteen or more hours a day), became fatigued easily, and had trouble getting up in the morning. I am still not sure why, but the doctors tell me that most people with vestibular problems have trouble functioning early in the day. I often could have stayed in bed longer, except I started feeling guilty that I should be doing something. Getting the rest you need, however, is an important part of recovering from, or coping with, any disability. I still need eleven or twelve hours of sleep a night, and I am insistent about trying to get it.

Be prepared for just about everyone thinking they

know a lot about your condition and offering their suggestions. I often hear that I should volunteer, or do a certain craft or get a job. Most of these things are not within my capabilities, and it really irritates me when I hear these comments. It's difficult to believe that people don't understand that I would be working, volunteering or going to school if there were any possible way for me to do so. In a way I can see that they are trying to help. It is just irritating that even people I don't know have some sort of advice (mostly unsolicited).

Comments about how lucky I am that I am okay and that I could be much worse off can be just as irritating at times. Somehow, it seems obvious to me that it could have been worse, but it seems to rarely occur to anyone that it surely could have been better. I am grateful that I wasn't injured more severely or killed; however, I still have a lot to deal with, and I often don't feel so "lucky." I would prefer that people don't pretend to know what I am going through by categorizing me as being lucky. I realize that it is probably hard to come up with something else to say at times, but if that is the case, I would prefer to hear a joke or a question rather than be preached at about how grateful I should be that I'm "only" disabled.

Then there are some family and friends who, though they mean well, are upbeat about every suggestion anyone has. Everything will be *the* thing that makes me better. They are of the mind-set that if you just work hard enough and long enough you can heal or "cure" yourself and whatever ails you. It is important for these people to realize that this is NOT always possible, and people aren't always supposed to try to push through things because that could, as in my case, cause their medical condition to get worse.

I think it is difficult for the people around me to understand that this is not something that I can recover from because I have "bounced back" from other situations previously. This is different. It is a permanent condition that, if anything, will get worse over the years (barring some medical breakthrough, which would be nice).

I do not hang my hope on anyone or anything any longer. If and when my healing happens, it will be wonderful to have my brain and body back. In the meantime though, there are times when my situation is terrible and anyone who tells me it isn't, has no idea of what I am going through or what they are talking about. They have no right to tell me how I should feel.

It seems everyone has some story to tell about a friend of a friend who went through a terrible ordeal and how great it turned out for them, so I should be doing whatever they did and I will be "cured." How in the world do they know — especially if they are not doctors, since even the doctors aren't sure. (If the information comes directly from a person who had a similar thing happen, then I am interested. If it comes from someone else, it is not always of interest or helpful.)

While it can be frustrating to talk to people, I also want others to know what it is like to be in my situation. There are so many things going on that describing one aspect of my illness doesn't come close to describing the whole situation. I am dealing with a physical condition, but I am also having to sort out my thoughts and deal with some unpleasant memories and feelings.

For example, the first horrible feeling I remember having after the accident was when I had to get in the car to ride from the hospital to my parents' house. I was afraid of everything: riding in a car, thinking about other people driving (especially at night and in the rain), etc. Just about anything scared me. I was always thinking of these horrible scenarios, worried that something horrible would happen to someone I cared about or to me, and how everyone else would feel. I'm not sure why, but I was usually more afraid of someone else getting hurt physically or emotionally (if I was to die or be hurt again, for example). It still bothers me.

Another difficult thing to deal with has been having a "different" brain than I used to. I used to remember things fairly well, and now I sometimes forget how old I am (and I don't even have that many years to remember). My body betrays me as well. My motor functions sometimes go berserk, leaving me unable to walk well, or stand still. Often when I want to do something, I can't. Small tasks such as stitchery or reading are difficult because of the coordination and concentration they require. Anything that requires physical coordination such as aerobics or even going for a walk or lifting anything is out of the question because of my physical limitations.

Sometimes even having dinner and talking with friends is enough to wear me out or make me physically ill because of the energy it requires. Being invited to parties is sometimes depressing for me because I want to be able to go and have a good time, but I know that, realistically, it is not always possible. It's difficult to explain to others what it's like to dread doing something fun because of the discomfort it will cause during the event and afterward.

Many people tell me that my illness is no different than one they have dealt with, and that I should not pretend that it is. But I basically have had to restructure my entire life. I know that there are many people who experience worse things in their lives, but that doesn't negate the experiences I am having to face. When I try to make plans for the future, I am not sure how to do it because I am unsure what my future will be like. My mind cannot forget dreams and plans, although my body may not know what it can do.

Sometimes the emotional toll an illness takes is as devastating as the physical one. It is difficult to feel sexy or attractive when you feel that you are at least 100 years old. The outlets I used to have to make myself feel better are now pretty limited. I used to love to go dancing or to aerobics, or just to dress up and go out somewhere without taking along a reminder of the illness (in my case, my cane). I have found that getting my hair done, or having a makeover are temporary ways to ease the feeling of being a "fossil," but they are usually expensive. Buying a new outfit is a good temporary reliever, too; however, it presents the same problem. My parents and Bill have sometimes sprung for one or both of these things, and that is a double treat.

Bill now has a more structured job, which is easier on me in some ways and harder in others. On the down side, I have to find other ways to get to places. On the other hand, it is nice to have a steadier income, more benefits for him, and a job that he can leave at the door when he comes home. When he worked for himself, he could determine his own hours, but he also had to constantly be thinking of what to do next, and where the next job would be, and if we could pay the rent. I am glad (and a little envious, I suppose) that he finally has a job in his field of study. I am happy for him, but it sometimes makes me feel that I am a failure, that I am not able to do what I set out to do. Part of this is that I am still grieving, and part of it is that I am having to find other things to boost my self-esteem.

Renewing a sense of self-esteem is a difficult

process. It is an area that is often overlooked when dealing with people who live life differently than the average population. A good example is in the medical equipment industry. I had to buy a cane to use, and most of them on the market are ugly. I don't know why someone can't come up with a line of medical equipment that is useful AND attractive. I finally chose one made of clear Lucite, and I attach colorful bows and ribbons to it for the seasons and holidays. Being twenty-four years old and having to buy a cane was a demeaning experience. It made me feel old and unattractive, and was very difficult to get used to. I am sure that there are other young people out there in my situation, and even older people who would be in the market for a more attractive walking device. I think it would be great to make a cane similar to the toys they have out now — a hollow one you could fill up with candies or one filled with glitter stars that move as you move the cane. Even different colored canes of various materials and designs would be appreciated. If it's the correct height, a handsome, carved walking stick with generous curved top could be useful and aesthetically appealing compared to a cane. Ideas such as these would make using a walking device much easier and enjoyable. Someone out there should start producing a more interesting and fun line of medical equipment. Many of us would benefit from newer, more attractive looks. (Professor Nancy Shuster may have the answer to the drab cane dilemma. She has formed her own company, Cane Coordinates, featuring colorful canes for every occasion.)

CONSERVING ENERGY AND ADAPTING TO A NEW SITUATION

(Check with your doctor about which changes are appropriate for you.)

Changes in Medication and Diet

- Eat small amounts of food throughout the day to keep your body nourished.
- Drink lots of fluids throughout the day.
- Take a daily vitamin and mineral supplement.
- Check with your pharmacist and doctor about possible drug or food interactions between any prescriptions you are taking.
- Cut back on or eliminate drinking alcohol. Alcohol can interfere with prescription drugs, and can be lethal in combination with medications.
- Take any prescriptions you may have at the same time each day.
- Have a pizza or another favorite food delivered when you are tired and don't feel like cooking. Don't feel obligated to eat everything if you have dietary restrictions. (For example, I pick off most of the cheese and meats on a combination pizza to reduce my sodium intake, but I can still share the meal with

friends.)

- Comply with all dietary restrictions that doctors recommend. Many restaurants now offer dishes with low salt, low fat, no MSG, etc.

- Keep water, a snack and any medications you will need to take during the night by your bedside.

Good Medical Practices:

- Keep a daily log of your activities, foods you've eaten and how you feel. This will help you and your doctors determine what has an adverse effect on you.

- Make sure you have had all recommended vaccinations. A yearly flu shot is a good idea, also.

- Have a routine physical examination, in addition to seeing any specialists. Other medical conditions may have an effect on your disabling illness.

- Have all of your specialists send copies of your medical records to each other and to your primary physician. Keeping a copy for yourself is a good idea as well.

- Write down your questions and observations to take with you when you have your medical appointments. You are less likely to forget to ask or tell the doctor something important.

- Have a routine eye examination (especially if you are visually dependent). Try to see an eye specialist who is familiar with your illness or disability; ask your specialist for a referral.

- Get a Medic Alert bracelet or necklace, and keep updated emergency medical information (doctor's phone numbers, prescription information, etc.) with you.

- Keep your medical information, family medical history, and insurance information with you at all times.

Physical Exertion: Lightening Your Load

- Do things a little at a time.
- Take breaks or naps whenever you feel you need to.
- Rest up for important events that you know will tire you, and be prepared to rest for a few days after the event.
- Alternate doing something that requires you to stand with something you can do while sitting.
- Have your hair cut and styled so that it is easy to maintain.
- Do only the recommended amount of exercise your condition allows.
- Some shopping malls offer use of baby strollers; get one to push your packages around instead of carrying them.
- Shop via the Internet for convenience. Several on-line "stores" are available, such as:
     http://www. netgrocer.com/.
These "stores" offer discounts and fast delivery of food and other needed items.

- Hold onto a friend's arm when going through crowded areas.

- Take along a cane that converts into a small chair (available at medical stores) or a collapsible chair that is small and easy to carry. Ask a friend to carry it for you if it is too difficult to carry.

- If dusting is too taxing, remove knick-knacks that collect a lot of dust. Keep them in a box until you feel you have the energy to clean again.

- Carry a smaller purse. Carry only needed paper money or debit cards, and not a lot of change.

- Maintain your ideal weight. (Ask your doctor what weight is best for you, and how to go about losing or gaining weight, if necessary.)

- Shop at times when there are likely to be fewer people in the store.

- Use a shower stool to take a shower sitting down.

- Raise your clothes dryer to reduce the amount of bending or stooping you have to do.

- Get the amount of sleep each night that your body needs.

Ways Others Can Help

- Tell friends and family members what hours you sleep so that no one disturbs you.

- Get voice mail or an answering machine and a telephone with a ringer that can be turned down or off. This will enable you to receive your messages without interrupting your sleep or resting periods.

- Arrange with friends to alternate cooking.

- Ask others to do cleaning that is too strenuous or that requires chemicals that give off unpleasant fumes.

- If you like to shop at malls but are not supposed to walk very far, or if you tire easily, wheelchairs can usually be checked out at the mall service desk or information center. Borrow or rent one, and have someone push you from store to store. Motorized carts may also be available for people shopping alone.

- Let others help with grocery shopping or things that are difficult for you to do.

- Get your hair washed at a salon or have someone help you.

- Have someone drop you off and pick you up at building entrances if there is no parking nearby.

Think Ahead

- Layer your clothing so that you will be comfortable in varying temperatures.

- Make grocery lists and get your coupons in order before going shopping, to allow you to finish more quickly.

- Wear earmuffs, hats and scarves on cold days.

- Wear shoes with low heels and/or shoes with support such as athletic shoes or boots.

- Wear earplugs when noises are too loud.

- Try using "noise cancellation" headphones when going to crowded places.

- Get a quieter hairdryer if noises bother you, or let your hair dry naturally.

- Wear sunglasses or a brimmed hat when it is bright out.

- Carry snacks with you. There may not always be food available and it is a good way to save money.

- Stay away from people with colds and flu. Wear a mask if it is necessary to be around sick people.

- When planning to travel or take a vacation, remember to plan for needed rest stops, and to take any needed medical supplies, prescriptions and any special pillows needed to make resting or sleeping more comfortable. Pack an extra pair of contact lenses or eyeglasses.

- When you are planning a trip, contact your destination (hotels, resorts, travel agent, attractions, etc.) in advance to ask about discounts and special arrangements for people with disabilities.

- If your memory is affected by your disability, carry a small notepad or electronic "memo-minder" with you to record things you don't want to forget.

DEALING WITH THE
MEDICAL SYSTEM

- Personal stories and feelings
- How to get in touch with the right people
- How to get good service

At some point after the car accident, I learned that the doctors had not told me everything about my injuries and condition. My insurance company called about one of my bills, and one of their questions revealed some information that I had never heard about. All I had been told by my doctors was that I had some cranial nerve damage (causing some facial drooping and numbness), and that I was suffering from inner-ear concussion syndrome. Through the insurance company, however, I found out that my skull had apparently been fractured and some of my sinus bones were damaged. No one had mentioned any of this to me.

I was angry at the medical personnel for treating me like an idiot and frustrated about being kept unaware of my total medical situation. I felt I had the right to know what my medical condition was, even if I didn't understand it all, so that I could do research for myself. I wanted to know what was going on, even if there was nothing I could do about it.

Sometimes you have to be rather insistent and persistent with doctors. Some of them get into the habit of telling you only what they think you need to know. This approach does not work with me, so I finally took it upon myself to get all of my medical records transferred to my primary physician. She now gets copies of all of my medical documents so that they are in one place, and at least one person knows everything that is going on with me medically.

For the most part, however, I have been lucky in that the doctors I have now understand my complicated symptoms and have worked to try to do something about them. I went through quite a few doctors before I found people that, I felt, were competent. (Several doctors told me that my symptoms would just go away in time. I even had one doctor tell me that if I just drank more water I would feel better immediately.) Although my current doctors may not have the answers, they are willing to keep trying and, at the same time, treat me respectfully.

In my search for doctors, I made inquiries to people throughout the country, and found that, by some strange coincidence, many of the people who knew the most about vestibular problems were located in my hometown of Portland, Oregon. These people travel extensively to educate other professionals about vestibular disorders, looking to teach as well as gather ideas from their colleagues around the globe.

Getting in touch with the right doctors is partially trial and error. Ask friends and family and your other doctors for referrals to people they trust. Ask around about doctors' reputations with patients, and ask about their specialties. Once you have an appointment to see someone, evaluate them yourself. Do they listen to what you say and respond accordingly? Do they explain what they are thinking and what procedures they want to do? (It's your body. Don't let anyone do something you don't think is necessary or you are hesitant about.) Get second and third opinions. Take someone with you on your office visit, and get their evaluation of the doctor. Sometimes a third party will ask good questions you may not have thought of, or will observe different things.

If you aren't comfortable with a doctor or have personality conflicts with him or her, don't go back. I had several doctors who told me my problems were all psychological and that whatever I was feeling would pass. Having enough information about my own medical situation, I was able to tell them that I would not be requiring their services anymore. That is never an enjoyable or easy thing to do, and it usually makes you feel as if you have been cheated out of valuable time.

Always ask questions. Become knowledgeable about your illness by getting as much information as you can, and keep abreast of the changes and developments in medical research. Go to the library to do some research. Use the medical library. Ask your personal physicians what they know. Find people in situations similar to your own and learn whom they recommend, and how they deal with different issues. The golden rule when choosing a doctor should be, "When in doubt, trust your instincts." If something or someone doesn't feel right to you, don't ignore that warning signal.

Several people have asked me what I think of the medical system based on my experiences. I am lucky in that I had already seen some of the inner workings of hospitals before my accident. I had family members who had worked in hospital settings since before I was born, I was accident-prone as a kid, I'd been a surgery patient several times, and I'd worked and volunteered in hospitals and studied physical therapy. I basically grew up in and around medical facilities.

Some of my previous experiences as a patient had awakened me to the fact that not all doctors, nurses and medical people are accommodating and friendly. They are not all there to help you. Some of them just want their paycheck and are not very interested in your well-being. I am glad I learned that early on, because it would have been a lot worse had I not known.

There are dedicated people out there who do want to help. They are just a little hard to find sometimes. When you do find them, make sure you let them (and their superiors) know. When you find someone who is rude or insensitive, the same thing applies-especially the part about letting their superiors know. Get in the habit of writing letters-letters of recommendation and appreciation, as well as letters of dissatisfaction. Be explicit in what you tell people. Give them concrete examples of both good and bad behavior. The people who are not giving adequate care should be reprimanded, and the people who go above and beyond their duties should be recognized and appreciated.

My view of the medical field has not changed that much, except I am now much more adept at dealing with discourteous people, and finding my way through the jerks to get to the really competent and caring people.

Don't limit yourself to traditional medicine either. If you want to see an acupuncturist or herbalist, it should be an option for you. Find doctors who are willing to work with alternative medicine, and who can warn you about potentially dangerous alternative treatments, and you will get the best of both worlds. If you think something might benefit you, it may be worth a try.

It can be very lonely if you are suffering from an illness that is poorly understood. You have to become your own advocate and find out what your options are. I had one "doctor" tell me that the quality of life one has will always be the same and it is all in your expectations. Although this has some truth to it, it can not, in my opinion, be accurate as a general statement. If I want something and have set my sights on attaining that goal, and I achieve it, I am happy. Then if something happens and all of a sudden I can't do any of the things that previously made me happy, my quality of life is NOT the same. It is true that I will learn to do new things and will, I hope, like what I am doing with my life again. But it takes some adjusting to deal with the bitterness and disappointment of losing what your initial expectations and achievements were.

I still believe that each life situation has some positive aspects to it, no matter how small they might be or what anyone else may tell you. The challenge is to discover what those aspects are, and to find facets of yourself that you never knew existed. Most importantly, emphasize the positive.

RELATIONSHIPS

- *How an illness can affect others*
- *Holidays and social events*
- *Deciding whom to talk to and how much to tell*
- *Thoughts on parenting*
- *Responses from a survey of friends and family*

A visible or invisible disabling condition takes its toll not only on the person with the disability, but on the people surrounding that person. Relationships inevitably change as people try to figure out their new boundaries and needs and where they see themselves in the overall scheme of your lives together.

Holidays and special occasions are among the times when I most notice the changes in my relationships. I used to be someone who enjoyed going to parties and talking to people, but now it's different. The parties that I often looked forward to are now somewhat unpleasant because of the noise and commotion. I don't have the energy to keep repeating to different people how I am doing without becoming exhausted and cranky, and I find that I have little else to talk to people about. I am not working or in school, often my life is not moving in any particular direction, and I get tired of talking about my medical problems.

Just as difficult is sitting and listening to all of the other people who are doing exciting things in their lives. I feel a bit envious at times. I keep having conflicts in my own mind, wanting to be happy for people, but knowing I am having trouble with it. I want to be optimistic and cheerful, but I don't feel that way very often, and I lack the energy to "appear" cheerful. Often, after about ten minutes of being in a room full of people, I have overloaded my circuits and need to sit somewhere quiet and try to regain my senses.

I've learned that, at times, family and friends may see me as being unhappy, angry or jealous — when in reality I just may not be feeling well. I imagine that, at times, I appear to be snobby or antisocial, but most of the time I am just uncomfortable and trying to deal with all that is happening around me. Although I am not able to enjoy family or social events the way I used to, I was unaware that I was sending out mixed signals in my mannerisms until I sent a survey to some friends and family members. Their responses convinced me that I should try to be more direct about how I am feeling (both physically and emotionally) at social events, and especially during the holidays, since they seem to be packed with things to do and people getting together.

All of this is especially difficult on my family and on Bill. They are frustrated when I am frustrated, and don't quite know what to say or do. They end up taking me to the doctor, the grocery store and wherever else I need to go, and they have had to change their lives in several ways because of me. They see me struggle and cry and turn white as a sheet when I've done too much. At times, that makes me feel bad for them, although there isn't much I can do about it, except try to be appreciative and thank them for what they have done for me. Despite all my frustrations with the world, with them and with myself, they have always been there, loving and supporting me, and that's all I can ask for.

Although it is sometimes hard to be honest and considerate with the people who know you best, always try to thank the friends and family members who help you most. These people do not have to do you favors, so when they do, try to remember to let them know their efforts are appreciated. On a similar note, rely on others for some things that you need, but don't take advantage of their efforts. Rely on yourself to keep as busy and as independent as possible.

I have not discussed the issue of how having children affects people with disabling and fatiguing illnesses. That's because I do not have any children. At this point in my life, I feel that I have enough to deal with in my own situation, and I do not think I would be physically or emotionally able to raise a child. Perhaps at some point in my life I will feel up to the challenge of having kids. I actually like the idea of children and seeing them grow and spending time with them, but the reality of the extra noise, responsibility, mental challenges and the multitude of other changes that would be necessary, is something I am not ready for yet. I am not even sure that physically I would be able to go through pregnancy and delivery.

I am sure that there are many people out there who already have children and are still dealing with issues such as mine, and I imagine it has to be even more difficult. The only advice I have is to try to get as much outside help as possible from friends and family, and to try to take time to care for yourself. Talk to people in support groups who also have children and see what their solutions are, and ask your doctors to assist you in developing your own ways of conserving energy and enjoying your family at the same time.

If you really want children and are dealing with a situation similar to mine, talk to your doctors. They can help you decide what is reasonable. You may also want to look into parenting preparation classes for people with disabilities. Don't rule out adopting a child, and no matter what you decide, consider hiring a professional nanny or working out arrangements with friends or family members to help you.

Even if children aren't an issue in your "new" life,

relationships with other people — friends, family and co-workers will be. I felt it would be valuable to get some information from friends and family about how they feel my situation has affected all of us. Although I originally thought of it as part of the research for this book, the results convinced me that it can be a valuable way for anyone to learn about themselves and the people they care about.

I sent out the survey to the friends and family members who have been closest to Bill and me. I asked slightly different questions of various people based on their "closeness" to the situation, but basically the surveys covered such topics as:

- What they feel has been the hardest thing for me, for Bill and for them to deal with concerning my situation.

- What they see as my strengths and weaknesses (and theirs) in dealing with the situation.

- How well they think they understand my medical condition and resulting limitations.

- Changes they have seen or sensed in me or Bill.

- Changes (positive or negative) in their relationship with me.

- Other changes in their life because of my situation.

- What advice they would offer me or someone in a similar situation.

Not everyone was able to respond (such a survey is not easy or quick to complete), but the responses that I received from about sixty-five percent of the friends and family members that I sent the survey to were enlightening and interesting. I understood most of the answers people gave, but was surprised on several occasions.

I found that many people commented on the difficulty in finding a balance between being supportive and encouraging, as opposed to being overbearing and meddling. It was also difficult for people to determine when I was feeling poorly. Some people said that if I had let them know in advance and reminded them occasionally when I wasn't feeling well, they wouldn't construe my being quiet and uninvolved as being rude, antisocial or snobby.

Most of my friends said that they did not fully understand my medical situation, whereas the family members were about evenly split. In some cases, the people who thought they understood were the people I would have said do not understand it very well. It was a good reminder that not everyone can (or will want to) understand someone else's medical problems entirely, and it is not always in your best interest to try to get them to do so. There will always be people who think that they know or understand more than they really do, and that is just something that we have to learn to deal with.

In my opinion, some of the best answers to the question about how well they understand my medical condition came from my parents and one of my friends. My friend said, "I believe that her situation is complicated but I understand it on a very basic level." My parents said that they did not understand my situation any better than anyone else. I thought that these were both very good responses in light of the fact that even the medical community doesn't understand my situation very well. Another good response was from a member of Bill's family, who said that "only Sharon and Bill can fully understand all the limitations, medical conditions and complications."

The hardest thing for most people to deal with about my situation was realizing I cannot be cured at this point, and that I am disabled (and all that goes along with that). Also, that I am relatively young, and have had a lot to deal with and adjust to physically and emotionally. They also said that it was hard not to be able to rely on me to do things and to participate in social events as I did before.

Most people thought that they had been both a positive and negative influence on me since the accident, and I would agree.

Everyone who responded to the survey said that they realize having to change goals, not being able to plan my life easily, losing my financial security, and losing the dream of becoming a physical therapist are the most difficult problems for me. One person said that they also recognize that other people's lack of understanding (as I don't look disabled) was difficult for me. (Right again.)

Many people said that they wished they could

have spent more time talking to me and trying to understand my situation (by the way, it's never too late). They also wished that they had thought about getting me out of the house more. Several people said that they did not know what they could have done differently because my situation is so unique and unpredictable.

My strong points in others' eyes were:

- Being realistic and practical, and being a problem solver.
- Being able to adapt to my new situation and find new goals.
- Being able to see that life can be meaningful and satisfying even if it is not going as originally planned.
- Being able to save money and develop new skills.
- Being strong-willed, independent, loving, courageous, and self-motivated in seeking out as much medical advice as possible, and applying for benefits, despite others' opposition.
- Having a positive attitude and maintaining a sense of humor and laughter in my life.

My weak points in others' eyes were:

- Being too strong-willed at times.
- Being drawn to routine and not being as open as

I could be to new ideas right away.

- Not putting on a better "face" during social events.

- Not telling people more matter-of-factly how I am feeling.

When asked if their lives had changed because of my situation, several people said that they are now more aware of how a life-altering medical situation can affect someone.

The advice people had for me or others in a similar situation:

- Continue to develop new goals, gifts and talents.

- Try to do the best you can given the circumstances. More important than your circumstances is how you respond to them.

- Don't be afraid to ask for help, and to reach out to other people.

- Take responsibility for your illness by becoming an expert on it, and educating others so that they can understand and be able to help you more.

- Try to keep a positive outlook and use spirituality as a foundation.

- Be open to new ideas, challenge yourself, and don't be afraid to make your own needs and desires known.

The things that people saw as being most difficult for Bill to deal with were:

- Feeling guilty, especially since my situation is not curable.
- The inability of either of us to plan our lives very far in advance.
- Dealing with the stress of my medical and emotional needs.
- Being far away from his family.
- My restricted activities and modes of travel.
- Having to be the primary bread-winner.

Bill's strengths were seen as:

- His fidelity to me in a difficult situation.
- His generosity and strength of character.
- His work experience, and ability to always make a living.
- His sense of humor.
- His ability and willingness to put my needs before his at times.

The weaknesses people commented on concerning Bill were that sometimes he is too work- or goal-oriented, and doesn't take enough time for himself. There was also some concern expressed about how he can express his disappointment, anger and gripes without adding pressure on me.

The survey helped me understand how others view my situation, and what concerns and input they

Relationships are very important to recovery

would like to offer. I found that, for the most part, people were very supportive of Bill and me. I felt that people understood our personalities, our grief, and how we deal with what we have been given, but I did not feel that anyone consistently understood all of the difficulties that both of us have to face daily. That, in itself, is good to know because now we can make even more of an effort to inform and educate others knowing that they want to be educated, and that they will love us no matter what happens.

SPECIAL CONSIDERATIONS FOR CHILDREN WITH INVISIBLE ILLNESSES

Please note that I am, in no way, an expert in this area. These are my observations and ideas from those who have children in this type of situation.

- Difficulties that adults don't encounter
- Ways adults can help
- Ideas for children who have "nothing to do"
- Stress reducers for children

It is difficult having an invisible condition as an adult, but children with similar illnesses have a tough situation as well. They depend on adults to tell them what to expect, how to handle situations and what to tell others. They depend on adults to give them support, understanding and ways to cope with what is happening to them. Often, the adults may not fully understand what is happening, so how can the children? Another problem for children is that they often do not have the vocabulary and understanding of what is happening in their bodies to explain what it feels like to friends, family and doctors.

It is my hope that the information in this book will give adults more information so that they can give children some of the tools they will need to get through these difficult situations.

Children often have even more pressure to "act their age," to play with friends, and to do lots of activities, but often their illnesses and disabilities don't allow them that luxury. They may get pushed into doing activities that they aren't physically or emotionally able to do by other children or adults because they look fine and don't have a visible "problem."

One way parents and friends can help children is to inform teachers and the children's friends and parents that the child does have an illness, and to explain how that illness compromises that child's ability to do cognitive tasks or physical endeavors. Give them some idea of what the child can do and what they like to do, and try to alleviate any fears that they may have about "catching" the disability or illness. If teachers or classmates would like more information about the illness or have questions about how it will affect their lives, ask your doctors if they would be willing to go to the school to talk to the classmates or faculty and staff.

Another way to help children is to learn as much as you can about their illness so that you can be supportive and help them to learn about themselves.

Don't mislead them into thinking they can be "cured" if there is little chance of that. Try to come up with activities that you can do together, or that the child can do alone if he or she is bored and having a particularly difficult day.

Things adults can do to help:
(Please discuss the appropriateness of these activities with a doctor before beginning).

- Have a computer outfitted for any special needs your child may have.
- Talk to doctors and therapists about physical activities your child can do; help them by joining in the activity.
- Make sure they have their special pajamas, toys, etc. available to them, especially on bad days.
- Set up a home-tutoring system for days that they can't go to school. You can do this yourself with help from teachers, or find an older friend who can come over to help, or hire someone.
- Find some simple chores that children can do to keep them involved and participating in household activities, and to keep them from feeling as though they are being "waited on."
- Check with a social services agency to see if your children can make place mats, ornaments or other decorative items for charities or hospitals.
- Identify local educational resource stores or teacher resource stores. Their employees can provide

good ideas and materials for science projects, fun things or other learning activities.

- Encourage children to watch educational children's television shows.

- Hang a bird feeder by a window and start bird watching together. Get some books on birds and identify which birds come to eat.

- If your child needs a special diet, help them to follow it by removing "tempting" foods that they shouldn't have.

- Remember to take them out of the house if you can and to some fun places, or if they are homebound, make the house more fun for them by allowing them to do some "outdoor" things inside. For example, set up a playhouse or a tent indoors, or let them ride a bike inside.

- Make holidays fun by doing different and special activities. Decorate the house to add some sparkle (review the "Filling Time" chapter.)

- Go to the library or a bookstore and get some books on your child's illness. These books can include even more ideas of things to do and ways to help.

- Let yourself rest and become rejuvenated. Schedule a "day off" when you have a friend come over to "baby-sit" while you do something fun for yourself, or just spend some time alone. Not only will you feel better, but you will have more energy and quality time to give to your family.

- Organize a support group for the adults and the

children (separately and together), or go to one that is available.

Specific Ideas for Children who have "nothing to do." *(Refer to "Things to do when you have nothing to do."Talk to your doctor about which ones are recommended for your child.)*

- Make cookies together.
- Color in coloring books or on paper.
- Watch cartoons.
- Watch a special video or television show.
- Use a "walkie talkie" to communicate with each other.
- Work on a puzzle.
- Do homework.
- Use a computer to play games or learn about interesting people and places.
- Have them write a story about their life, their illness, a wish or a dream. If they can't write, have them tell it to you or talk into a recorder or make a video.
- Play a board game or cards with them.
- Invite a friend over to talk or spend the night.
- Read a fun book or listen to a tape or (parents/friends) read a story to them.
- Do some type of craft (drawing, stitchery, making sculptures out of clay, put together a model, etc.)
- Play with a pet.

- Make paper snowflakes or paper dolls.
- Write a letter to a friend, or identify a pen pal to write to. Again, an alternative to writing would be to tape record messages to people and have them send tapes in return.
- Play with rubber stamps and paper punches to make cards or stationery, or just a pretty picture.
- Make beeswax candles. Ask adults for help if you need to.
- Listen to music.
- Plant some seeds or bulbs and watch them grow. Help your child water the plants and take care of them.
- Come up with your own "things to do" list.

Holiday activities:

- String popcorn for Christmas tree garland.
- Make an ornament out of paper or other craft items.
- Help wrap presents.
- Help make and/or decorate cookies.
- Monitor the baking process by watching a sand timer and letting someone know when time is up.
- Hand adults decorations as they need them.
- Help with holiday mailings by applying stamps, return address labels or holiday stickers.
- Be in charge of keeping holiday music playing.

Stress reducers for kids:

- Squeeze and pound clay into different shapes.
- Draw or paint "mad pictures" to show feelings.
- Use puppets to reenact a scary situation or angry feelings.
- Hit a blow-up punching bag.
- Have a "safe" room where kids can say anything without getting punished.
- Do some exercises (check with doctors first) such as jumping on a trampoline, dancing in the living room, etc.
- Go to children's counseling or group sessions.
- Go to an illness "camp," if one is close by.

HOW TO RESPOND

- *Tough issues that disabled people encounter*
- *Responding to others and responses from others*
- *Common questions from others*
- *New friends*
- *Tips to alleviate feeling awkward during interactions with others*

I know that it's a long, lonely road out there for people who have visible disabilities. There are many obstacles to overcome. People tend to stare, and can be rude. Sometimes I experience those reactions when I am walking with my cane. It can make a person feel very old and vulnerable. My cane makes it apparent that I have a disability, but many times I appear quite normal. Some of the hard things that occur with an illness that can't be seen are the same as for those that can. Everything takes a lot of energy, most people can't and don't want to understand the depth of the disability, and you are constantly wondering what to tell people if they ask you about what happened. Do they really want to know, or do they want a positive, simple answer?

The invisibility of some illnesses such as mine causes some unique problems. If you appear normal and healthy, people think you ARE normal and healthy. People are more likely to perceive you as lazy if you aren't constantly doing something. They expect you to be able to do what they can do. Even after you explain your limitations, they may forget about them because you look normal and are doing a good job of masking your symptoms and discomfort.

Sometimes I am tempted to tell strangers something totally different than what the truth is. If they ask, "Did you hurt your leg?" sometimes it's easier and better just to say yes, rather than explain the real story. I think this is okay sometimes, if, for no other reason, than to give yourself a chuckle.

I am not usually one to go around complaining, and sometimes I don't assert myself. I carry too much, physically or mentally, because I don't want to explain again what I am not able to do, and also because I want to do some things I can't. It's tough to know who to tell things to, and how much to tell them, and how often they need to be reminded. You don't want to nag them, but you also don't want to keep hurting yourself by not saying what your limitations are. That is something I think that everyone has to figure out for themselves. Decide which people you feel comfortable divulging your complicated story to. Give others just a brief explanation and leave it at that as you probably won't see them that often. Or, as I do, keep them apprised of your situation in an annual Christmas card. That way, they know what and how you are doing, in general.

Occasionally, my friends or family will ask me questions about my accident, or ask me to describe how I feel about certain things. If they are sincere in their questioning, I am almost always willing to try to analyze myself so that we can both learn more. The best defense against ignorance is education. When you feel you are ready, educate your friends and family about what is going on with you. You both will probably benefit, even if it is difficult to tell them things initially. It helps if you have a family that is willing to learn and hear what you have to say, but if you don't, let your friends know your situation. At least then you will have someone who can sympathize with some of the things you are going through.

A common question people ask me is, "How would you like people to react to you, and what sort of questions would you prefer people to ask, so that they don't appear rude?"

The type of comments that are usually annoying are suggestions on what I should do or how I should cope with what I am going through. Most people have no idea of what my situation is. People who tell me to go to this doctor or that healer, or eat watermelons for two months (because that helped their twice-removed cousin by marriage when they were sick) are annoying to me — mostly because the person hasn't taken the time to find out what my situation is, and also because it seems as though they have not thought before saying something. I would rather not hear all of the stories about other people and their friends and how this or that cured them unless those people REALLY are, or have been, in a situation similar to mine.

Comments such as, "You are so lucky you don't have to work like the rest of us," or "I would love to stay home all day and do whatever I want instead of going to work," or "You are so lucky you get to do crafts and fun things all day," imply that having a disability or illness is fun, and that the disabled really CAN do what they want when they want to — which is generally not true. "Why don't you..." questions, and "You should try...," and "My friend did... and it really helped...," comments assume that I am stupid and have not thoroughly looked into treatments and ways to deal with my illness. The people making these comments assume that I am lazy or have given up, and that I know less about my situation than they do, which is usually far from the truth.

I would much rather have someone say, "I don't know if this is relevant to you, but have you tried...?" I don't mind people asking questions so that they understand things better, such as: "What happened to you?" or "Why are you walking with a cane?" or "What are your symptoms like?" because this type of question conveys that whoever is speaking is concerned about me. I do mind unsolicited suggestions: people telling me what I should watch, what I should eat, that I should get out of the house more (these are usually the people that rarely, if ever, offer to take me anywhere), or which doctor is just the right one for me. I also do not think it is necessary to tell me how lucky I am to have insurance, how many doctor bills I have or how much a trip to the doctor costs. I already know the total cost is high and there is nothing I can do about it. It only serves to make me feel bad.

People who tell me, "You should ride the bus and be more independent," or "You really should try not to depend on people," obviously don't understand what I am facing. I would rather they ask, "Why can't you ride the bus?" or "What do you do to stay more independent?" The way and tone in which a question is asked often makes the difference between a friendly inquiry and a rude comment. As a good friend, David Gonzales, once put it: "People who think they know it all are a legend in their own minds," and are usually not important to the people around them.

Right now, some of you are probably starting to get upset with me for pointing out some of the things that can be bothersome for the disabled to hear. You might be feeling guilty and angry at yourself because you have just read all of the things that you have told someone before. You might even be wondering if I was quoting you. But before you get defensive, take heart in the fact that just about everyone has made one of these comments at some time. The idea is that once you realize you have made a comment like this before, concentrate on NOT saying it again. To a certain extent, people such as I expect these comments from others, and one of the purposes of this book is to inform and educate you about different, more tactful ways of communicating and interacting.

Instead of advice, for example, I'd suggest you offer the disabled person something more useful: "taxi service" for an errand or a day, help with cleaning or household chores, a home-cooked meal or dinner out, a letter or "care package" in the mail, or a surprise visit or phone call. When you're taking a day trip or running errands, see if they want to come along. Do some reading or writing for them if that is difficult for them. Take care of a chore for them. Put together a homemade "coupon book" with coupons for rides to the grocery store, a massage, a day or evening of company, etc. Do something or send them something anonymously.

Sometimes people respond to a disability in surprising ways. It is gratifying when strangers who pass by me say something such as, "I like your cane," or "That is neat the way you decorate your cane." Sometimes I get asked if the cane is a present for an "over-the-hill party." One child saw my cane and yelled out, "Hey! That's a pretty cool cane!" I thought that was a pretty neat thing for anyone, but especially a child, to say. I also got a chuckle out of a little girl who was interested in why I had to use a cane. I explained to her, in terms that a four-year-old could understand, that I had been in an accident and had hit my head, and I had trouble walking because I was wobbly. Her eyes got really big and, in a very excited voice, she asked me if she could see me wobble! Most of the time I can laugh about whatever comments people make and explain that the cane is mine. Sometimes, after hearing my reply, they are embarrassed for asking. Sometimes they deserve to be — depending on what the comment was. For the most part, however, I don't mind people acknowledging my cane, or asking about it.

In my efforts to learn new ways to interact with people, I have tried to make new friends and talk to people in situations similar to mine because their reactions to me are not based on a previous relationship. A year or so ago, I met a young woman I had known in high school. She had been in a serious car accident and had been paralyzed. Later, I decided to try to contact her by letter. I wasn't sure, at first, if she would be interested in hearing from me since we were never close in high school. However, she did respond, and we have developed a friendship by mail. Talking to her through letters, I have found that we have a lot in common — mostly in our feelings and experiences in dealing with people. We both are unsure about people who knew us before our accidents because we are uncertain how they will respond to us. We have both had positive experiences and negative ones, and we are able to empathize with each other about the recovery and life-long adjustment process inevitable after a serious injury.

I find her very inspiring. She had taken it upon herself to find fun things to do, and not to feel sorry for herself. She has competed in the Paralympic Games and is trying to do the most that she can in her life. Although our situations are different in some ways, we have both talked about the way that people treat us differently after seeing us again. Most people just don't know what to say, and focus on what you can't do. Some try to pretend that nothing has changed, and some ignore you completely. Then there are the people who respond by being direct and asking how things are going, and what happened. It is awkward for both people when the person you run into chooses any other way than being direct to approach you. Some people might be scared that they will offend me by asking about what happened, but I find that, for myself, and people I know in similar situations, we are usually happy to explain if the questioner is sincerely interested. We will tell you if we are uncomfortable.

A relative of mine had a son who was in a serious car accident about a year after mine. She told me that some of his friends who hadn't seen him after the accident were afraid that the would find him grotesquely disfigured. Showing them a recent snapshot of him relieved their anxieties. Some sighed in relief and said things like, "Gee, he looks like he's okay," or "He still looks like himself!" After that, she said, they called and visited him more often — much to his delight.

As far as people I know well responding to me differently, I haven't had too many weird reactions. Most of the people whom I see and am around now are people that I see regularly (friends and family that are close by). My friends around the country only know about my disability through my letters. From the letters they have sent, they feel bad for my losses, but they probably don't have much more reaction than that. I have had the opportunity to meet some people from high school whom I haven't seen for awhile. Most of them just want to know what happened, but some try to avoid me altogether. I would prefer that they ask questions rather than looking at me across the room with no contact. Sometimes I am afraid of how people will respond, but there is little I can do about it, so I try not to let it worry me.

Alleviating Awkwardness During Interactions With Others

- Don't feel compelled to tell everyone everything about your situation. Tell your friends and people whom you feel comfortable with more, and simplify the situation for everyone else.

- It's okay to make up a story to tell strangers who ask you about your illness or disability. Just don't go overboard. Keep it simple and lighthearted.

- Instead of waiting for someone to ask you about what happened, start off by addressing the issue yourself. This may alleviate some awkward initial moments of conversation, especially to those people whom you are meeting again in life.

- Inform your friends and family that you would rather them ask you questions about what you can and can't do, instead of making their own suggestions, or "telling" you what they think you should do (give them a copy of this book with this section earmarked).

- Prepare visitors in advance about your situation, especially those people who haven't seen you in awhile. Let them know your limitations, things you are uncomfortable with, and any physical devices you use, or physical changes in your own appearance that may take them by surprise.

- Tell people that you don't mind answering their questions. If you are uncomfortable talking about anything, let them know that as well.

SEX AND BODY IMAGE

- Sex is not a four-letter word
- How to acquire and keep a positive body image
-Specific difficulties and problems disabled people might encounter
- Tips on improving your body image and your sex life

Sex. It's not even a four-letter word, yet many people (including me) have a difficult time talking about it. I considered avoiding writing about the topic altogether, but it is an important, and often difficult, part of life (especially for people with disabling illnesses). Besides, someone has to bring up the issue, so it might as well be me.

There have been a lot of books written entirely about sex, so I'm not going to pretend to cover all of the issues. There are, however, additional issues that people with illnesses have to face.

One of the obvious difficulties I see is the issue of sustaining a positive body image (being satisfied with your appearance, weight and size). This is hard enough for people without disabilities, but it is an

-84-

enormous obstacle, at times, for people who have limited options available to improve their physical self and their self-perception. Exercise is a good way to start feeling better about your body, but many of us are not able to do much exercise. Any physical therapy that is recommended for you is a beginning, but there are other things you can do as well.

Begin to exercise your mind by thinking positively about yourself. Identify something you like about yourself (even if it is a fingernail, your hair or your little finger), and focus on the fact that there are parts of you that you find attractive. Try to add more things to your list and emphasize what it is you like about yourself. Stop the negative thoughts that many of us bombard ourselves with in our own minds. Quit saying to yourself that your thighs are fat and ugly or that you hate your butt (or whatever it may be), and try to replace that thought with a positive one: "I look pretty good in this pair of jeans," or "I like the color of my eyes." This may not come easily; I have to work on it every day. But if you do have a "beat yourself up" kind of day, don't beat yourself up the NEXT day for beating yourself up. Just start over again, thinking positively.

There are many books available on how to achieve a better body image. Go out and get some and use the tips they offer. Once you start feeling better about your body and yourself, you will feel sexier, more comfortable and less inhibited.

The effort it takes many of us to get through the

day is so overwhelming that it often leaves little or no inclination to think about being romantic. Many medications cause lethargy, sleepiness, and sexual "numbness" or apathy. Talk to your doctors about these symptoms if you experience these problems, and they may have some solutions to increase your libido.

My friends ask many questions about my disability, but it is the brave person who asks about sexual issues. One friend of ours, after hearing that I can't exercise or do any sort of strenuous activity, blurted out quite candidly, "What about sex?" It is a good question. My answer was that we have to deal with and accept some of my constraints that limit our physical relationship, develop less strenuous ways of lovemaking, and create a romantic mood at a time during the day or evening when I have more energy. Sometimes the exertional "rules" are broken and I pay for it for the next several days. This can create another problem by turning a positive experience into a negative one, so if you do "break the rules," be careful not to make it a habit that reinforces how awful you will feel and cancel out the pleasurable experiences.

If you are unsure of how to be "creative" in your sex life, first talk to your partner. If you are both at a loss, go to the library or bookstore. There are numerous books that can help give you new ideas. There are even some books about sex and sexual issues written exclusively for people with disabilities.

Sometimes the burden of your illness will completely turn you off to sex. In this case, it helps to have a loving, patient partner who will not pressure you, but it may become a significant problem in your relationship. Ideas for help might be to talk to your partner and family about how you can get more rest (see "Ways to conserve energy and adjust to your new situation" in the "Difficult Adjustments" chapter), talk to your doctors about any solutions they might have, and consider getting some counseling for each of you to understand your situation better, and, in some cases, to teach both of you new and different ways to have a meaningful sexual experience together.

Tips to Develop A Positive Body Image

- Exercise if you can, or do physical therapy exercises.
- Eat a healthy, well-balanced diet.
- Do "emotional exercises" to pump yourself up.
- Stop thinking about yourself negatively or vocalizing your negative thoughts about your body.
- Tell your partner and friends that compliments (sincere ones) are nice to hear (and contrary to what some people believe, you will not get a "swelled head" by receiving compliments).
- Find books or books on audio tape that offer advice on achieving a positive body image.

- Go to a seminar or class on body image improvement.

Tips For A More Satisfying Sex Life

- Think more positively about yourself and your body.
- Talk to your partner about your feelings and fears, and any changes that have occurred while dealing with your illness or disability.
- Find books that offer new ideas and more advice.
- Go to a seminar or a support group to get ideas from others.
- Try counseling.
- Talk to your doctors about your difficulties. They may change some medications you are on or give you other helpful solutions to any problems you are experiencing.

FINANCIAL CONCERNS

- Applying for disability benefits
- Getting through the paperwork
- Finding individual and government programs
and benefits
- Transportation issues
- Ways to conserve money

If you find yourself in a situation like mine in which it seems inevitable that you will have to live with what you have, go ahead and cry for awhile, but then get down to business. An issue you will need to deal with is your financial situation.

Sometimes I feel bad that I can't contribute more financially to our household, but I do what I can to even out the balance. I try to keep our apartment clean, and make dinner when I can, but it still puts a lot of pressure on Bill. I often feel that I am not doing enough, although I am probably attempting too much at times.

There is some assistance out there. Although it can't give you back your old life, it can help you with your new one.

Check out the government programs in your city and state, and apply for disability benefits. Initially, my parents did not like the idea of my applying for these benefits. I didn't much like that option either, but at some point you have to decide to do something to help yourself, even if it is not the option you wanted. Look in the blue pages or reference portion of your phone book for a place to start. This is a lengthy process — it can take up to a year or longer to get results.

What usually happens is you talk to a social security person and have an initial phone interview. If they determine you are eligible for benefits, they will send you the paperwork. The paperwork may go back and forth for awhile. If they can't decide if you are eligible based on what you've told them and what your medical records tell them, they may have you see one of their own doctors for an evaluation. This physician will ask you questions about your illness and abilities, and then send a finding to the case worker assigned to you. After a review, you will be notified as to whether or not you are granted benefits. If you are, they send you a statement and explanation of benefits, as well as information about when your case will be reviewed. If you are not, you are given a chance to appeal the decision if you wish.

Families can also begin this process of applying for benefits if their loved ones are unable to do so themselves. It shortens the wait, and is one less thing for the patient to worry about during recovery.

People who are eligible for disability may also be eligible for other assistance, including Medicare or Medicaid. Social workers can help place some disabled people in appropriate jobs. (Read the Americans with Disabilities Act. It will help you understand how not to be discriminated against, what actions employers must take to accommodate workers with disabilities, and many other issues that concern people with disabling conditions.) Some phone companies offer discounts to people with disabilities as well.

Talk to the department of motor vehicles about getting a handicapped parking sticker; that will allow you to park closer to medical offices, stores, restaurants and other places.

Your particular illness and restrictions will determine the type of parking permit you are given. Because I don't drive, I have a small cardboard placard that I take with me when riding with others. There are also permanent license plates and stickers available to people who are able to drive.

I had several student loans that were coming due soon after I quit school because of my condition. I informed the loan company about my situation, and was able to qualify for a dismissal of my loans because of my permanent disability. Again, however, this can be a long process.

Don't expect things to happen too quickly and you won't be disappointed. I got through the waiting period thanks to my family. They helped me financially and also let me live with them so I didn't have to pay rent. When I finally decided that I was able to move out with Bill, we inquired about renters' assistance. We should have done this earlier, because we found out that there was a six-month waiting list. Luckily we found a place to live that we could afford without the assistance.

To keep from spending more than our budget allows, I shop at places where things are less expensive. Outlet stores, discount stores, garage sales and thrift stores are all good places to find things. Some things may need a little repair or sprucing up, but if you have the time and skill to do that, your money will go further.

WAYS TO CONSERVE MONEY:

Using Coupons and Rebates

- Use coupons, double coupons, and store discount cards if stores offer them. Send in rebate forms.
- If you don't get a newspaper, have friends who don't use coupons save them for you.
- Send in for the free things you see on cereal boxes, etc. and give them as gifts to children you regularly give gifts to.
- Buy coupon books offered by nonprofit groups for discounts on food, entertainment and shopping

items.
- Buy discount tickets to the movie theaters.

Shopping Strategies

- Shop at thrift stores, discount stores, garage sales and volume/bulk stores if they are cheaper.
- Compare store prices for things you buy often.
- Stock up on items you need when they go on sale.
- Don't buy something just because it is inexpensive. Buy it because you need/want it and it is a reasonable price.
- Buy second-hand items and fix them up instead of buying things new.
- Buy a vehicle through repossession sales or rental car auctions.
- Investigate buying a home or car through government seizure programs.

Reuse and Recycle

- Take old books or audio tapes back to a second-hand store for credit to buy new books or tapes.
- Have a garage sale.
- Reuse wrapping paper, bows and boxes. Or use maps or newspaper comics as wrapping paper.
- Take old clothes to a resale store or swap with friends.
- Trade your unwanted but usable items with

friends for their unwanted or usable items.

- Reuse picture frames after getting tired of an old picture.

- Use both sides of writing paper.

- Save metals such as copper and aluminum and take them to a recycling company for cash.

- Trade in unwanted gold or jewelry for cash or credit.

- Borrow exercise equipment from a friend who is not using it, or consider a low-cost membership to a gym. There are also some stores that trade, buy and sell new and used exercise equipment.

- Use rechargeable batteries.

Gift-Giving Strategies

- Buy gifts in advance when they are on sale.

- Set a limit on how much you will spend on gifts for holidays and birthdays.

- If you receive a gift that is not your style, save it to give as a gift to someone you think will really enjoy it.

- If you are overwhelmed with buying holiday presents for every family member, talk to them about choosing names so that everyone will only have to buy one gift. Set a limit on how much money can be spent.

- Remember people who are worse off by donating to reputable charities, even if it is only a few dollars. It makes you feel good, and helps others.

- If you already own a family heirloom or something that you know someone else would like, give it to them as a gift.

Be A Careful Consumer

- Cancel credit cards that charge an annual fee. Try to get credit cards that offer cash rebates or other bonuses.
- Try to pay off high-interest credit cards first, and then try to use your cards as little as possible. Instead use cash, check or a debit card.
- If you are overwhelmed by your financial situation, contact a nonprofit organization and ask for some financial help. Many organizations offer free financial advice and counseling.
- Do research before buying. Call around to compare prices (but remember that your time is worth money, too).
- Realize your budget constraints. Don't try to compete with friends.
- Try to save some money each month for emergencies, big-ticket items, or special gifts.
- Don't get fooled into something that sounds less expensive but, in reality, is no deal. It is sometimes more expensive, for example, to have a piece of furniture recovered than it is to buy a new one. Buying bulk items is not always cheaper either. Check the unit price.

- "If it sounds too good to be true, it probably is." This old saying is a true one. Avoid get-rick-quick schemes, telephone and mail scams. Read the fine print. Check people and businesses out before investing or buying. Use common sense when reviewing ads and offers.

- Sell some antiques or valuable items that you no longer use or want.

Entertainment and Holiday Savings

- Make your own holiday ornaments and seasonal decorations with things you have around the house. Ask others for ideas.

- Cut your own Christmas tree and decorative greenery.

- Make your own wreaths and garlands.

- Rent movies instead of going out. Watch movies with friends, and alternate who pays.

- Tape movies on television to watch later.

- If you have cable television, the movie channels occasionally have free "preview weekends." Watch these movies or tape them for future entertainment.

- Make holiday goodies instead of buying them if it is cheaper to do so and if you enjoy doing it.

- Host a Tupperware or similar party. The host usually gets some free merchandise. Friends may be willing to help with food, set up, etc.

Reducing Household and Food Costs

- Pack your family lunches, and eat at home more often.
- Establish a reasonable budget and stick to it. Allow money for fun stuff.
- Swap favors with friends. Example: Make your friends the cookies they like in return for a ride to the grocery store.
- Write letters instead of making long-distance calls. Or use e-mail.
- If you have friends who can get free or discounted items through work or connections, barter with them for something you have or can make.
- Accept others' gifts graciously and thankfully. (Always send thank you notes!)
- Buy stamps from grocery stores if they offer a discount on stamp booklets.
- Cut back on paper items like plates and napkins. Try to use reusable ceramic plates, washable napkins and glasses.
- Use free greeting cards and address labels that come in the mail.
- Get a "green plug" for your freezer or refrigerator. It will help reduce your electric bills.
- Turn lights off when you are not using them. Use night lights instead of overhead lights when appropriate.
- Wear sweaters in winter, allowing you to save

on heating costs, and dress lightly in summer.

- Send parcels by third-class mail instead of first-class.

- Share clothes if you have friends who are your size.

- Have a pot-luck dinner.

- When you have something to sell, advertise cheaply. Put up your own signs, use word-of-mouth, and reputable newspapers to advertise in.

- Invest in insurance (renters' insurance, car insurance, health insurance, life insurance, etc.). The initial cash outlay will be well worth it if a catastrophe occurs. Be careful not to get scammed. Buy from reputable companies and check with the Better Business Bureau if you still need some guidance.

FILLING TIME

- What breaks up the days
- Dealing with boredom
- Planning your day
- Support groups
- Changing your surroundings
- Things to do when you have nothing to do

So how do I get through the days? Well, some are awful and some are okay. Bill plays an important role in keeping me sane. He has been there through all the ups and downs, and he is probably the only other person who really has a good grasp on what my ailments and my restrictions are. He is good at sensing when I am not doing well or feeling well. He is very patient, jokes with me and gets me out of the house, even if it is just to do errands. We watch home movies and generally just have fun together. Having him around simply makes things easier most of the time.

I also became reacquainted with an old friend from high school and his wife. The four of us have become good friends, and they are both extremely conscientious and available for anything I might need. In fact, they help a lot more than they probably realize, and I have been lucky in having them as friends. They are also willing to take me places and do fun things to break up the days, as are my parents and sister, now that they understand my situation better.

But some days I am just plain bored, and there is nothing I can find to calm myself down. I just feel as though I have ants in my pants (and not just ordinary ants — more like giant RED ones). I can't find anything I want to do, and I get tired of watching television. There is absolutely nothing that will help me to feel better. So what do I do when that happens? NOTHING! I just have to wade through those days and feel miserable, doing a few things here or there, cleaning up the dishes, etc., just to keep my mind from going crazy. I have no magic solutions for these times. Sometimes days like that are just going to happen, and there is not much you can do about it.

These days are difficult physically because there is nothing to get your body moving, and your muscles are not doing anything. They are even harder emotionally because this is when you REALLY miss your independence. I can't tell you how many times I've wished I could drive or get myself somewhere. All I can think about is all of the things I want to do but can't. I wrack my brain for someone to call, or someone I can ask to go do something with, but my mind is blank...except for extreme frustration with my entire situation. The funny thing is that, if you can get through those days (or weeks), the very next day you find a million things to keep you busy.

Sometimes just going to the doctor breaks up the day a bit, although it's not exactly what you'd call a good time. I try to keep myself busy doing things such as baking cookies, watching TV or writing letters. It takes me about three times as long as it once did to do these things, but it is something to do. Most anything I do I have to do in small spurts: fifteen minutes of baking, then rest. I try to write to my friends so that I will get mail (sometimes the highlight of my day). I create things to do, for example, organizing my filing system or making a list of people to send Christmas cards to even if it's July.

Going to the movies is fun, but sometimes the sound is too loud. I am not able to filter out sounds very well, so everything comes at me at once, and my system can't handle it, and I shut down. I usually take a pair of earplugs wherever I go. If I am stationary, I can use them, but I have found that if I am moving and put earplugs in, the pressure difference causes me to be more off balance, so I have to decide which is worse. I have also had to learn to just stop and rest and stay in one place for awhile so that I can adjust to my surroundings. This is particularly useful after being in a place with a lot of people or a lot of things such as the grocery store. After a certain amount of time I just need to sit down or wait in the car until the people I am with are finished.

I have learned that I need to plan what it is that I will do during the day. If there is something that will take a lot of energy and time, and it is something I want to do, I have to consider whether or not it will be worth it to be laid up for the next few days after doing it. Not many people can understand that. They think that if I am well enough to go to a friend's house one night to make cookies, that I always feel that well, and I should be able to clean and cook every day with no ill effects.

It would be nice to be able to look through magazines or books and get new ideas about how people with illnesses and disabilities stay in shape or lose weight. Unfortunately, most fitness books and magazines on the market are geared to able-bodied people. All of the diets and weight programs assume that people can exercise and that they burn a normal amount of calories and need a normal amount of calories. No one has addressed the issue of people in my situation, and who could blame them? Disabled people do not constitute a majority of Americans, but I am sure that there are people out there who could benefit from a plan from a dietitian, a physical therapist, a biochemist specializing in nutrition and metabolism, an exercise physiologist and a physician who could deal with the issues I have spoken of.

Most hospitals have several support groups available to people who are interested. Check these out. I went to a vestibular support group several times to hear some speakers, and also to get other people's input. In my search for a good group, I attended many where I knew more about the topics than the speakers, and much of the verbal exchange between the people there sounded like whining. I currently attend a support group that is composed of intelligent and caring people, so don't give up searching for a good group, if you want one. For many people, support groups are a great source of comfort and help.

One of the things that I do to keep my surroundings changing, and to keep my spirits up, is make an extra effort to make the holidays special, not just another run-of-the-mill day. A lot of people don't understand why I enjoy the holidays so much, or why I make much of them, but, for me, they are something out of the ordinary to focus on. They are a few days each year that I can try to make magical.

I try to remember birthdays and always send at least a card to the people I care about, and usually a little something to go along with it, because I know I would like someone to remember me and send me something. I make an extra effort to get Christmas and birthday gifts throughout the year for the same reason. It usually brightens the receiver's day, as well as my own.

I like to decorate for and celebrate special

occasions (even if only by having something different for dinner). I will wear green on St. Patrick's Day and do something special for Bill on Valentine's Day. I decorate the house differently for each season and holiday. And I always allow myself to enjoy the process of decorating, or the excitement of picking something out or making someone a gift, even if it is a small and inexpensive one. I like to be remembered on my birthday and special occasions, so I try to do for other people what I would like to have someone do for me. Sometimes I am criticized for going overboard, but I do it for myself.

I am always thinking ahead for birthday and Christmas gifts. I have a list of people (both in my head and on paper) that I want to buy or make gifts for. Each time I go out, I try to remember that list, and that way I can get someone something special early in the year and on sale.

A lot of people don't know where to get started to decorate their homes. I grew up in a household that was very holiday-oriented, so I come by it naturally. Say Valentine's Day is coming up. Pull out everything red, pink, white or heart-shaped that you own, or anything with angels, cupids or anything that is special to you from a previous Valentine's Day. Buy some red and white candies and put them in a dish. Put a red or pink tablecloth on a table. Trade your everyday knick-knacks for angels and Valentine mementos. Put red, pink or white candles in your candlesticks. Make a wreath or sign for your door. Put a heart garland around your door or in a window.

The same goes for any other holiday. For Halloween and fall, use fall colors. Pull out the fall candles, knick-knacks, potpourri. Get some fall candies for your candy dish. Do an arrangement of fall-colored silk or real flowers. Use hay and wheat and small pumpkins and decorator squash and corn (most grocery stores have them for a good price) for a centerpiece.

Of course, Christmas is a major holiday for most people. Don't be a grump. Get a tree and decorate it. Even if you don't have many decorations, be creative. String popcorn. Make your own ornaments. Wrap small boxes like packages and put them on the tree or under it. Hang your stockings somewhere. If you don't have a stocking use a real sock (preferably a clean, dry one). Decorate with red and green and white. Take a day and put on Christmas music and wrap some of the presents you've gotten in advance.

If you never had holiday traditions as a child, make some of your own. Go out and cut your own tree, or make a fun trip of going to pick one out. Let everyone have a say in which tree they like best and in deciding where the tree will go when you get it home. Have a popcorn-stringing or cookie-making party. Play Christmas music. Go see "The Nutcracker." Visit the streets that have lights on all the houses. String lights of your own. Whatever you do, decide to have fun and enjoy the new traditions you are creating.

THINGS TO DO WHEN YOU HAVE NOTHING TO DO
(Consult your doctors about which of the following are within your capabilities.)

Traditional Chores

- Dust.
- Clean out your refrigerator.
- Do small loads of laundry and folding.
- Make the bed.
- Split up daily chores such as ironing, making the bed and straightening the house, and list them on a calendar.
- Wash dishes.
- Pay the bills.
- Balance your checkbook.

Not-So-Traditional Chores

- Water plants.
- Clean out a closet or drawer.
- Make a grocery list.
- Clip and organize coupons.
- Plan your meals.
- Keep up on your filing.
- Straighten out the fringes on your rugs.
- Set up and use a home recycling center.

- Clean your light fixtures.
- Put shelf liner in drawers and cupboards.
- Change the batteries in your smoke alarms and other appliances.
- Wash clothes that need hand-washing.
- Replace burned-out light bulbs.
- Clean the stove or microwave oven.
- Wash windows and mirrors.
- Shave fuzzies off of sweaters.
- Give your plants a milk bath or clean their leaves.

Safety

- Make your house or apartment safer. Get a fire escape ladder, fire extinguishers, smoke detectors, carbon monoxide detectors, etc.
- Plan emergency escape routes.
- Put together a natural-disaster kit.
- Make a written or photo/video inventory of everything you own for insurance purposes.
- Get a safety deposit box.
- Child-proof your home (door latches, electrical outlet covers, etc.)

Paperwork and Organization

- Organize photo negatives.
- Go through old files and clean out what you don't need.

- Go through clothes and jewelry and donate unwanted items to charity.
- Organize a messy drawer.
- Organize your clothing and sock drawers.
- Put old notes and papers you want to save in three-ring binders. Glue small pieces to colored paper and make a collage to add to the binder.
- Send in rebates.
- Make a budget and keep track of your expenses.
- Save your change and cash it in once a year to buy something special or use it for emergency cash.
- Copy recipes and organize a recipe box.
- Sort your magazines by date and year.
- Keep a calendar and write your appointments and activities down.
- Get a new address book or update the old one.
- Work on applications for disability benefits, etc.
- Organize your tapes, CDs or records.

Correspondence

- Find a pen pal.
- Write letters to people you haven't heard from in awhile.
- Make a Christmas card list.
- Sign up for free catalogs or literature.
- Sign other people up for catalogs they would like.
- Try to respond to every letter you get.
- Write letters of praise or dissatisfaction to

doctors, nurses, etc.

- Call people you haven't talked to in awhile.
- Make a list of friends and family birthdays and send them cards.
- Send an anonymous letter of apology to someone you've hurt.
- Send away for freebies.
- Make your own cards. Use rubber stamps, colored pens and paper, magazine pictures, etc.
- Let people know you like to receive mail.
- Go through your mail.
- Send thank you notes.
- Use a cassette tape recorder to record a spoken letter to someone.
- Write a poem or love letter and give it to someone.

Special Occasions and Gifts

- Make a list of gifts you would like to give people for Christmas.
- Decorate for each holiday and season.
- Make a "wish list" for birthdays and Christmas.
- Think of gift ideas for people for special occasions (catalogs may help).
- Put wrapping paper and bows in containers that you can get to easily.
- Collect gifts for others on sale throughout the year.
- Wrap presents.

- Send holiday cards (Valentine's Day, Mother's Day, Father's Day, Easter, birthdays, Halloween, Thanksgiving, Christmas, etc.).

Things That Don't Require Much Effort

- Look through old photo albums.
- Look through magazines.
- Have someone read to you.
- Show or watch a movie on videotape.
- Look through catalogs.
- Take a nap.
- Look through recipe books for new ideas.
- Have friends take you with them on errands.
- Read a children's book.
- Watch your favorite television shows.
- Get a barometer, and track how you feel as the barometric pressure changes.
- Just sit, relax and think.
- Sit outside on a beautiful day.
- Order stamps by mail.
- Play old records, tapes or CDs.
- Make hand shadows on a wall.

Psychological Pick-Me-Ups

- Take a long bath.
- Take care of your skin. Use lotion after showering.
- Get a haircut, have your nails done or get a

makeover.
- Invite a cosmetics representative for a demonstration.
- Dress up just for fun.
- Adopt a pet.
- Keep a few toys to play with (no matter how old you are). Ideas: Etch-A-Sketch®, coloring books and crayons, puzzles, etc.
- Hug a stuffed animal (take a favorite with you for overnight hospital trips).
- Make appointments with others to do fun activities (movies, shopping, dinner out, etc.).
- Be around people and things that make you happy.
- Color with crayons.
- Meditate or pray.

Games and Hobbies

- Look into playing "virtual baseball" or sports.
- Take up a hobby like stitchery, painting, drawing, collecting or knitting.
- Make cookies or brownies.
- Play games on a computer (this may not be a good option for visually-dependent people or people prone to motion sickness), or play card games such as solitaire.
- Try origami (the Japanese art of folding paper).
- Take photos.
- Do crossword puzzles or word games.

- Sing or play an instrument (or take music lessons).
- If you have access to a computer, play games, write letters, do research, explore the Internet, etc.
- Put together a puzzle.

Activities That Require More Time or Effort

- Put pictures in photo albums, or put dates and names on the back of photos.
- Become a teacher's aide.
- Read books or listen to books on audio tape. If reading is difficult for you visually, try placing a colored transparency over the page. Some people with vestibular problems find it easier to read through a colored transparency rather than directly from a white page. Experiment with different transparency colors.
- Make a tape of songs you like.
- Make a video if you have a video camera.
- Rearrange the knick-knacks in your house.
- Keep a daily journal of your thoughts and activities.
- Put framed pictures out for people to see.
- Put out silk or real flowers and change them occasionally.
- Take a walk.
- Enter sweepstakes.
- Invent an easier way to do something.
- Do some research about your particular illness

(use the Internet, get books at the library, etc.).
- Do your exercises or physical therapy.
- Try to overcome a bad habit (biting nails, etc.).
- Educate your friends and family about your illness and keep them updated on how you are feeling, both mentally and physically.
- Join a support group.
- Volunteer somewhere.
- Submit a recipe in a contest or to a magazine's cooking section.
- Invent a new main course or dessert item by trying new ideas.
- Cook bacon the old-fashioned way.
- Research your family tree and lineage.
- Try to record family stories from parents or grandparents on tape or in print.
- Change tablecloths and linens on end tables and dinner tables for a new look.
- Take a class on a subject that interests you.
- Come up with your own "Things to do when you have nothing to do."

SPIRITUALITY

- My personal thoughts
- Options to help achieve inner peace

I am not a person who believes only in one group or type of "religion." I see many good lessons, thoughts and teachings in most of the traditional religions, but I prefer to use bits and pieces of each of those, as well as lessons I have learned from good and loving people, to guide me along my way and give me faith.

Whether you are someone whose beliefs are similar to mine, or if you have embraced one particular "religion," I believe that it is important to find peace within yourself and with others, and learn to see the goodness in each possible situation.

A structured religion can offer many things such as support groups, a place of prayer, and, most of all, something good to believe in and an example of goodness to follow. It can also be a good source for things to do: support groups, helping on committees for various outreach programs, retreats, etc.

If you do not wish to be involved in an organized

or established religion, I still encourage you to look for the good things in life. Draw upon all of the positive things you see around you, and learn from people who are honest and trustworthy.

Any kind of hope and faith you have will help you to get through your situation — especially your darkest days. So use whatever methods of prayer, meditation or spirituality hold appeal for you.

Several friends and family members have tried to "encourage" me to go to church and to "pray" in the way that they do. I would rather they understand that I have my own beliefs and value systems, my own way of being spiritual. Just because I don't attend a service doesn't mean that I am not a good person or that I don't believe in a higher power or energy. I know many people who go to church often, but are still not very considerate to others. I would prefer to learn from anyone and anything that teaches love and good will and incorporates those ideals into life.

It is easy to question why something happened to you. There have been times that I was sure that this was my punishment for any little thing that I had ever done wrong in my life. Although there are still moments when this idea flashes into my mind, I think I am well past the point of making up for the mistakes I have made, and that we all make, in life. I believe that everything happens for a reason, and although it may take a long time to understand, there is still an explanation. Perhaps I would have been unhappy as a physical therapist, or Bill and I would have never met under different circumstances. It's possible that I now have the time and opportunity to become a better person than I was before all of this happened. Maybe I will be able to touch more people's lives now than I would have otherwise. I don't know the answers to all of my questions, but I believe that the unpleasant experiences I have survived have brought me where I am for a good reason.

I recently came to appreciate a situation that, at the time, I thought was devastating. When I was in high school I was diagnosed with a severe case of mononucleosis (mono). I was out of school for about three months, and in bed for most of those days. I was not sure I would be able to graduate with my class, but I was tutored at home to keep up. I was forced to quit the volleyball team I had played on for two years, and also had to stop rehearsing for a play I was in. I couldn't understand why all of it was happening to me. I believe now that that particular situation was preparation for learning how to adapt to and overcome difficult situations. Had that not happened to me before the accident, I think that I would have been even more emotionally devastated and less able to cope with all of the changes that I have had to face.

I prefer to believe that even in the most horrible situation, there is something positive that will come of it. I hope that I will be able to see the positive outcomes of bad situations that happen, but even if

I don't, my belief in basic goodness helps me to sort out and deal with the bad things that are happening around me.

Before I decided to become a physical therapist, I was interested in clinical psychology. I learned early on that you don't have to be certifiable (insane) in order to benefit from some therapy. While I was in the process of going to medical doctors and trying to figure out what was wrong with me, I also went to a therapist on several occasions to sort out my thoughts and emotions. Don't close yourself off to this idea or the idea of couple or family therapy. It can be a very beneficial part of your emotional recovery and a way of finding inner strength and peace.

HINDSIGHT

- *My outlook after my experiences*
- *Some funny and strange recollections*
- *Old traditions and new ideas*
- *Final comments*

One of the questions I have been asked is, "How has your situation changed your outlook on life?" The answer is that sometimes I am a more positive person, and sometimes I am more negative. I am generally more relaxed and patient with the world, although it is difficult to be patient in specific situations because of the tremendous effort it requires to do so. For example, it is difficult to take care of someone else who is sick or injured because my system overloads so easily. I worry a lot more about everything. I am often scared that my life, or the life of someone close to me, will be cut short at any time, so I am grateful for the time that I have and try to live each day as if it were my last.

I think I am more conscious now of telling people what I am thinking. I try to thank people more. I try to spend more time with people and not say anything

I would regret if I never saw them again. I try to tell more people that I love and appreciate them. I always try to tell Bill I love him when he leaves and when we go to sleep. I try to tell my family more often that I love them also. I have experienced being close to death, and losing many meaningful things. Now I want to try to enjoy the time I do have, and keep my regrets to a minimum.

Some of the things I remember and don't remember about the night of our accident are interesting and funny. Bill and I do not know how I got out of the car or how long I was unconscious. I do remember having to go to the bathroom REALLY badly and not being able to go — partly because the medical personnel didn't want me to move my neck, and partly because, although I tried to go right there on the table, I couldn't! I remember being insistent about not wanting my clothes cut off of me. I kept telling the medical team that I could take my own clothes off. When they began cutting I was really mad because I had just bought the jeans I was wearing (hey, they cost $40!), and I was wearing a red sweater that I had borrowed from my sister. I was certain she was NOT going to be happy about that! (Despite the old joke, however, I never once thought about whether my underwear was clean or not.) I also remember thinking that I had wanted a way to get out of taking my organic chemistry test, and that this certainly was ONE way, but not the way I would have chosen.

I remember that it took weeks to get all of the gravel, dirt, grass and grime out of my hair; looking around at the accident scene later, I couldn't figure out how so much gunk had gotten in there. I was not allowed to look in a mirror for at least a week (so as not to shock myself), so my parents took pictures of me in the hospital. At the time it wasn't a very appealing idea, but now it is somewhat interesting to look at myself in those photos.

I also remember a guy coming in next to me who was in some sort of motorcycle accident and needed some stitching as well. After they sewed him up, he asked if he could smoke, then he got up to call a friend, telling him that he just had a frontal lobotomy and would someone please pick him up!

The second day I was in the hospital, my grandmother and her brother sent me a special gift. When I was young I had a special teddy bear that I loved to play with any time I was at her house. The poor little thing had gotten so ratty and worn from love that all of the stuffing in its neck was gone. After I got older, the teddy bear got loved more by my cousins, but I always remembered it and had asked my grandma if I could have it some day. She agreed to give him to me if I would come over for a visit and some soup (a tradition when going to grandma's). I was in the accident before I had a chance to visit, but my uncle took the bus all the way across town just to give me that bear, along with a note that read, "Soup would have been an easier way to do this, you know!"

The night of the accident I remember thinking that maybe there wasn't really a gash in my forehead — maybe it was just a large indentation, although I realized I was bleeding. I remember being calm through the entire ordeal and cracking jokes to try to make Bill feel better. I remember my aunt and sister almost passing out after coming to see me in the hospital on the night of the accident. When I had the reaction to the codeine after coming home from the hospital, I remember the way my sister held our dog, Muffin, in the kitchen while about eight people from the fire department (they reminded me of the "Eight Stooges") tried to figure out how to get me out of the house and to the ambulance; they eventually used a chair because they couldn't get a backboard through our hallway. I remember the nurses telling me to be quiet as I was writhing in pain, and my dad yelling at a few people to get some action. I remember how scared I was and worrying about Bill, perhaps more than I was worrying about myself.

As I look back, I also recall changes in my relationships, such as with my parents. The months that Bill and I were living with them were a particularly challenging time for us. At times, we both felt that we had no privacy (as I'm sure my parents did as well), and I felt trapped, as if I would never be able to live on my own again. Bill had the additional stresses of living in a family other than his own, and trying to adapt to the interactions of people he would have never been living with otherwise.

On the other side of the coin, however, it was a time for my parents and me to get to know each other as adults. This was sort of a rocky process, but I think that, although the days I spent with them were some of the most difficult days I have had, that time has enabled me to become closer to, and have a better relationship with them. It also allowed my parents to get to know Bill and vice versa.

Because of the unusual living arrangements with my parents, I was a little surprised at their responses to my survey question of, "How has your life changed because of Sharon's situation?" Both of them said that, although it was a little difficult to adjust to the living situation, they thought it was a "pretty good time" that brought everyone closer and allowed us to understand each other better.

My situation has also given me a new appreciation for many of the things my parents did with us, and for us, as kids. Because I am no longer able to fly in an airplane, I am glad that my parents took my sister and me traveling when we were younger (although sometimes I think I'd be better off if I didn't know what I was missing). It helped that my dad worked for an airline, but my parents were always interested in introducing us to new places, and showing us cultural differences throughout the world.

I am also grateful that my parents were always conscientious about celebrating the holidays and including us in each occasion. Not only did it make life fun as a child, but it has also given me experience in how to make certain days special. Each holiday gives me something to prepare for and look forward to, which, as I have mentioned previously, is extremely important to me now.

My parents always made (and still make) an effort to make each holiday special, especially Christmas. Mom would always have the house decorated and smelling good with food and pine trees. Each year, a "Christmas tree cutting" day was marked on the calendar. We would drive out to a Christmas tree farm and walk around (sometimes for a long time) until we all agreed on a tree we liked. We'd cut it down, carry it to the car, and then it was off to get hot chocolate and donuts, and proceed home to decorate the tree. To and from the tree farm we would sing Christmas carols, and we would always have some holiday season music playing while we put the tree up and decorated it. Although the tradition now is to eat a more nutritious breakfast than donuts, the Christmas tree cutting day is still a tradition that we embrace fondly, all going out together to get the trees for our homes.

My parents' tree is decorated solely with homemade ornaments. They started that tradition when they were first married and had little money. Dad would cut shapes out of wood (candy canes, Christmas socks, etc.), and mom would paint them. They made ornaments out of Styrofoam, glitter, pine cones, and various other things. My sister and I started contributing ornaments at a young age (the ones we made in grade school usually hang toward the back of the tree now). That tradition still continues. Each year, mom and dad still make at least one ornament for their tree, and they make one for my sister and me for our own trees as well.

Now that both my sister and I are adults, we have created some of our own traditions to add to some of the ones we grew up with. We still have a Christmas celebration at my parents' house. We always have a party with our extended family to celebrate as well. Bill and I have also started a new tradition by watching "Scrooge" on Christmas Eve together (something from his past).

I try to mail Christmas cards at some point during the season to keep our friends updated on all that has taken place during the year, and Bill and I always try to spend some time with family and friends. We also set aside some time alone with each other. Each year, I try to give a handmade gift to at least one person (every year dad would make each of us something out of wood, and mom would sew us something). For me, it depends on how I'm feeling and how much time I have in advance to put into making the present. In previous years I've done stitchery, stockings, homemade ornaments, fudge or cookies, quilts, and, more recently, cakes.

Looking forward to and preparing for the holidays is something that helps me get through the difficult times. If I can keep my spirits up, the easier it is to deal with the difficult days I have had and that I know will follow.

I also look for inspiration in the people around me. When I was working at the hospital and volunteering, I came into contact with many people who amazed me. They were able to smile although they were alone on Christmas, or muster up thank you notes for all of the people working with them, although they had just been told that they would die soon. The traumas and difficulties these people were able to work through and come to terms with were incredible. I often took solace in the fact that they were able to do it, and wondered many times if I could be so gracious in a situation similar to theirs.

Now it is my turn. Every day I think about those people and how I want them as my role models, but often I don't quite measure up. There are days that everything hurts, including my soul. As much as other people try to be supportive, many times it is still lonely, and it feels as if I am charting new territory by myself, as though I am in the middle of a jungle. But I always try to find laughter in something and happiness somewhere and hold onto it because, usually, after a time, it will get me through anything.

As you look for a way to "get through" your life-altering situation, here are the main things I would encourage you to consider:

- Give yourself time to adjust and grieve.
- Realize that you will have bad days, bad weeks, bad months, and some unexpected setbacks (so I guess that means you can expect them).
- Find supportive members of the medical community to help you.
- Try to keep searching for the positive things in life — open some new doors for yourself, and don't close yourself off to others.
- Remember that your family and friends can be a great source of support if you educate them about your situation and how you are feeling.
- Be careful of letting your "pride" get in the way of helping yourself. Most people don't give "handouts," they give gifts or help because they want to. Allow them to help you if they wish to. Gracious thanks and acceptance of what is offered will make everyone feel better.
- Try to keep a sense of humor about yourself and your situation. It's amazing what can be funny when you are looking for humor in what seems to be quite a serious situation.
- Don't make excuses. As my grandma told me, "Your friends don't need them, and your enemies will never believe you anyway!"

If you keep these things in mind, your life may not be the same as before, but maybe, like me and Julio Iglesias, you will find that your life can still be rich and rewarding.

APPENDIX 1 —
MY FRIENDS AND
FAMILY SURVEY

As I was preparing to write this book, I felt it would be important to gather some information from friends and family about how they feel my situation has affected all of us. I sent a letter and survey questions to a variety of family members and friends. The results convinced me that it can be a valuable way for anyone to learn about themselves and the people they care about.

The cover letter I sent with the survey read:

Dear friends and family,

I am trying to gather research in the form of opinions and experiences of the people who have been around Bill and myself, and who have experienced in one way or another all of the things we have been through in the past several years.

I am hoping that the information you give me will help other people in similar situations and allow them to relate to the experiences you and I have had. Please try to be as honest as possible (even if it means describing a negative experience). These are your perceptions and opinions and they won't be valuable unless they are truthful. Take some time to think about what you want to say, and then return it to me. Also, if you can't answer or are not comfortable answering a question, or it does not apply to you, feel free to leave it blank or say that it is not applicable. Thank you for your time and feedback.

The questions I sent to Bill's friends and family were:

1. In your opinion, what have been the hardest things for Bill to deal with concerning Sharon's illness (and both of them having to do things differently than they originally planned)?

2. In your opinion, what have been Bill's strengths in dealing with the situation?

3. What do you think Bill sees as being his weaknesses (if any) in dealing with the situation?

4. Do you have any concerns about either Sharon's or Bill's future, and/or their future together?

5. Do you think that you understand Sharon's medical situation and all of the limitations that she and Bill have to deal with?

6. What changes (if any) have you seen or sensed

in Bill during the last four years?

The questions I asked of my own friends and family were similar, but geared more toward how I've changed as well as how my situation has affected their lives:

1. What was your first reaction/impression after realizing Sharon had been in an accident?
2. How has your relationship with her changed: both for the better and for worse?
3. What has been the hardest thing for you to deal with about her situation?
4. Do you think you have had a positive or negative influence on her during the time since the accident?
5. What do you see as having been the greatest obstacle for her?
6. What would you like to have done differently in your interactions with Sharon since the accident?
7. What do you think Sharon's strong points and weaknesses have been in dealing with her situation?
8. Has your life changed because of Sharon's situation?
9. What would be your advice to her now, or what advice would you give to someone else in the same situation?
10. Do you think that you fully understand her medical situation?
11. Describe how your feelings about her situation

have changed in the years since the accident.

12. Do you have any longer term concerns about Sharon's future?

13. What have been the hardest things for Bill to deal with in your opinion?

14. In your opinion, what have been his strengths and weaknesses in dealing with the situation?

APPENDIX 2 —
SURVEYS YOU CAN USE

If you think your family or friends may be uncomfortable sending their comments directly to you, have them send responses to someone who is willing to retype them and give them to you confidentially.

A. Questions for your partner's friends and family.

1. In your opinion, what have been the hardest things for _____'s partner to deal with concerning his/her illness?

2. In your opinion, what have been _____'s strengths in dealing with the situation?

3. What do you think ____ sees as being his/her weaknesses (if any) in dealing with the situation?

4. Do you have any concerns about either ____'s or ___'s future, and/or their future together?

5. Do you think that you understand _____'s medical situation and all of the limitations that

he/she and his or her partner has to deal with?

6. What changes (if any) have you seen or sensed in _____ during the last __ years?

B. Questions for your own friends and family.

1. What was your first reaction/impression after realizing _____ had been in an accident or discovered he/she had a disabling illness?

2. How has your relationship with him/her changed, both for the better and for worse?

3. What has been the hardest thing for you to deal with about his/her situation?

4. Do you think you have had a positive or negative influence on him/her during the time since the accident/ illness? Why?

5. What do you see as having been the greatest obstacle for him/her?

6. What would you like to have done differently in your interactions with _____ since the onset of the illness or accident?

7. What do you think _____'s strong points and weaknesses have been in dealing with his/her situation?

8. Has your life changed because of _____'s situation?

9. What would be your advice to him/her now, or what advice would you give to someone else in the same situation?

10. Do you think that you fully understand

his/her medical situation?

11. Describe how your feelings about his/her situation have changed in the years since the onset of the illness or accident?

12. Do you have any longer term concerns about ____'s future?

13. What have been the hardest things for ____'s partner to deal with in your opinion?

14. In your opinion, what have been his/her partner's strengths and weaknesses in dealing with the situation?

15. Comments:

C. Questions to ask yourself.

Just as a survey of friends and family can be a learning tool, so can answering some questions yourself, and having your partner answer some questions as well. By answering the following questions, both of you may realize things about yourself that may help you in your situation and that may be helpful to share with others in your life.

1. What has been the hardest thing for you to adjust to about your new situation?

2. What types of activities or situations would you now prefer to avoid?

3. What would be helpful for other people to know about your feelings?

4. Explain what type of illness or disability you have as if no one had ever heard of it before. (This

might help you, as well as people you share this information with understand exactly what your medical situation and limitations are.)

5. What would be a good day for you?

6. What would be a bad day for you?

7. Do you like people to visit you in person, or would you rather talk on the phone or communicate by mail/e-mail?

8. What do you feel has been your greatest loss and why?

9. What positive things have come out of your situation?

10. Explain what your physical pain/discomfort feels like, and how your situation makes you feel emotionally.

11. What types of things or situations frighten you now that did not before?

12. What things make you feel more at ease?

13. What question or comments do you hear that make you angry, annoyed or sad?

14. What things do you miss doing?

15. What have you always wanted to do, but now may not be able to?

16. If you have visitors, what is an ideal length of time for them to stay before you tire? Have you let them know that?

17. Do you mind talking about what has happened to you, or would you rather avoid the subject?

18. How many hours do you sleep each day?

What time do you go to bed? What time do you wake up?

19. Do you take naps during the day?

20. Are you a "morning person" or a "night owl"?

21. What are your favorite activities?

22. What household chores do you find most difficult?

23. What do you do to keep yourself occupied? How do you overcome boredom?

24. Do you have a "comfort food" or something that makes you feel good?

25. Do you enjoy social events or parties or would you rather avoid them? Is this a new attitude or has it changed since your illness or disability?

26. What do you see as your strengths?

27. What do you see as your weaknesses?

28. How have your relationships with people changed for the better or worse?

29. Are you optimistic or hopeful about your future? Why?

30. What things do you want to try to do in the next year?

31. What things do you want to try to do in the next five years?

32. What things do you want to try to do in the next ten years?

33. What things do you want to try to do in the next twenty years?

34. How well do you understand your medical situations and your limitations and requirements?

35. Whom do you have the most trouble communicating with or relating to?

36. Is it difficult to see people who knew you before your illness or disability?

37. Comments:

D. Questions for your spouse or partner.

1. How has your life changed because of the illness or disability of your partner?

2. What has been most difficult for you in this new situation?

3. How has all of it affected your relationship with your partner's family?

4. If your partner's situation makes him or her less independent than he or she would be otherwise, how has this affected your relationship?

5. What advice would you offer someone else who is married to, living with, or in a relationship with someone in a similar situation?

6. What, if anything, would you like to see your partner doing differently in response to his or her situation?

7. In what ways are you (or would you like to be) involved in the medical decisions your partner makes (such as which doctors to see, which course of treatment to follow, etc.)?

8. How do you cope with your negative feelings regarding the situation? How are your own needs being met?

APPENDIX 3 —
VESTIBULAR DESCRIPTIONS

Many people with vestibular problems have a hard time explaining the sensations that they are feeling. Often the only way they can describe it is "dizziness," or feeling that "the room is spinning."

I have come up with descriptions of the different sensations that I feel and have tried to put them into words. This has helped me let people who have not experienced these sensations (doctors, family, friends, etc.) better understand the condition. I feel it also helps me (and may help others with vestibular conditions) give physicians more help in determining exactly what part of the vestibular system is creating the symptoms.

Sometimes I feel as though I'm...
    ...walking on stilts.
    ...walking through thick fog.
    ...spinning to the left or right.
    ...spinning in zero gravity (can't tell which way I'm spinning, tilting or turning).

..."drunk."

...moving in slow motion ("Reverse Warp Speed").

...moving in fast forward.

...tilting.

...lightheaded.

...unable to coordinate any of my movements.

...continually watching a really long, poorly-filmed home movie.

Sometimes I feel as though I...

...have the flu (sweating, nausea, or feeling as if I will pass out).

...have blinders on.

...have motion sickness.

...have a hangover (nausea, heavy head, foggy).

...just got new glasses (I feel really tall and can't coordinate my feet).

...am about ready to pass out.

I sometimes feel as if...

...my head is very heavy and "full," as though it weighs a ton.

...the room is rocking, spinning or tilting at an angle.

...my eyes are spinning or bouncing around in my head.

...my eyes are "jerky" when I move them.

...my vision is "out of focus" or "fuzzy."

...I'm on a roller coaster.

...the room "bleaches out" so that it is hard to see color or focus on anything.

...everything takes an extraordinary amount of time and energy.

...my head, brain or eyes (or any combination of these) are falling and turning at the same time (like beginning to fall into a spin).

...my head is detached from my body.

...my head is on a spring (bouncing around uncontrollably).

Other sensations I experience include...

...a slow-motion rocking, as though I'm on a boat.

...a time lag when I move my head before my eyes catch up with whatever I am doing.

...a "Lava Lamp" motion.

...not being able to look up or down without feeling as though I am falling forward or backward (or actually doing so).

...seeing everything as a sea of moving colors and shapes, all blending into one another.

APPENDIX 4 —
REFERENCE LIST

For the names of good physical therapists with training in the treatment of vestibular disorders, contact your personal physician or VEDA.

Vestibular Disorders Association (VEDA)
P.O. Box 4467
Portland, Oregon 97208
(503) 229-7705 or (800) 837-8428
Fax (503) 229-8064
http://www.vestibular.org
http://www.teleport.com/~veda/
e-mail: veda@vestibular.org

Pacific Northwest Sleep/Wake Disorders Program
1849 N.W. Kearney, Suite 202
Portland, Oregon 97209
(503) 228-4414
Fax (503) 228-7293

Medic Alert Foundation
P.O. Box 1009

Turlock, California 95381-1009
(800) 432-5378
http://www.medicalert.org

Noise Cancellation Technologies, Inc.
One Dock Street
Stamford, Connecticut 06902
(800) 278-3526
Fax (203) 348-4106
www.nct-active.com

Cane Coordinates
Professor Nancy Shuster
Unit 1015818 Glencove Drive
Naples, FL 33963
941-597-2932 or
79 Boon St.
Narragansett, RI 02882
401-789-8783

APPENDIX 5 —
BASIC EAR ANATOMY AND
DETAILED INFORMATION
ON MY PHYSICAL
THERAPY EXPERIENCE

SOME BASIC EAR ANATOMY

The first thing I'd recommend (if you don't already have a good concept of ear anatomy) is to find in a textbook or in an anatomy software program a picture that illustrates the ear in some detail. You will see that the inner ear is made up of a bony "labyrinth" that contains the membranous labyrinth. The membranous labyrinth consists of thin sacks and tubes that carry two types of fluid: endolymph and perilymph.

Each inner ear contains three semicircular canals. Each canal is sectioned off by a cupula. The cupula contacts hair cells, which are sensory receptors. The fluid and cupula in the semicircular canals move every time your head moves. The hair cells bend with the direction of the movement and send an impulse to the vestibular nerves, which, in turn, tell the brain, along with input from your visual system and proprioception, where your head and body are rotating in "space."

There are also two chambers in the membranous labyrinth: the utricle and the saccule. Within each of these chambers is a bed of hair cells coated with a layer of gelatin containing crystals called otoliths. This entire structure is called a macular organ, or macula. The macula in the utricle responds to horizontal linear motion of the head, and the macula in the saccule responds to vertical linear motion of the head. As your head moves (actively or passively), the otoliths are pulled in the direction of the earth by gravity. The gelatin layer moves with them, bending the hair cells in the direction of the movement. When the hair cells are bent, they stimulate sensory nerve endings to send an impulse to the vestibular nerve and to the brain. This is the vestibular system in action.

The brain stem is the main part of the brain that coordinates balance. It is constantly receiving input from the visual system, muscles and joints and the vestibular system. It then responds to this input by sending out motor nerve impulses to different muscles, allowing clear vision during movement and the ability to balance ourselves by controlling different muscles in the body. When one of the three major input systems is damaged, the information from each system that is sent to the brain may conflict with one another, which may cause "dizziness."

PERILYMPH FISTULAS

I have referred to perilymph fistulas as "holes" in the membranes that separate the inner ear from the middle ear. More accurately, an "inner ear" fistula is a tear in the round window, the oval window, or both. In my particular case, I have tears in both membranes and in both the left and right ears. These tears allow fluid from the inner ear to leak out into the middle ear. This disturbs the normal pressure of the inner and middle ears and may cause dizziness and even hearing loss.

Having fistulas makes the inner ear susceptible to pressure changes (such as altitude) that would normally only affect the middle ear. This direct pressure can cause unhealthful stimulation of the vestibular system and the hearing structures, therefore increasing unpleasant symptoms. Some of these symptoms include nausea, vomiting, dizziness and imbalance, tinnitus, hearing loss and a fullness, or sensation of blockage, in the ear. People with fistulas should not do any exertion or activity that would increase abdominal, chest or head pressure because the increased pressure will transmit to the inner ear. Fistula "precautions" include, but are not limited to:

- No lifting of over five pounds.
- No pushing or pulling of anything weighing over five pounds.
- No flying in airplanes.
- No swimming or scuba diving.
- No jumping out of airplanes, bungi jumping or riding or carnival rides.
- No strenuous exercises.
- No bending over.
- No straining on the toilet.
- No nose blowing
- No standing on chairs or ladders.

Some of the symptoms experienced because of fistulas are also symptoms of endolymphatic hydrops. In a healthy ear, the endolymph remains fairly constant and nourishes the sensory hair cells of both the vestibular and hearing structures. The systems that regulate our blood composition and fluid levels in the body do not normally affect the level of endolymph in the ear. However, when the inner ear has been damaged, the regulatory systems do affect the endolymph levels in the ears, causing large fluctuations. Pockets of endolymph can shrink and swell drastically, causing the sensitive hair cells to become abnormally stimulated.

Hydrops can be "managed" with a diet that focuses on keeping the fluid volume, level of sugar and salt concentration more consistent. This usually involves eating more frequent but smaller meals (rather than three large meals) and cutting back on high-sodium foods. Doctors also recommend limiting or excluding caffeine and alcohol from the diet, as both contribute to changing fluid levels in the body.

My diagnosis consists of bilateral fistulas, bilateral hydrops, general inner and middle ear damage due to the head injury, some brain stem injury, sleep apnea and restless leg syndrome.

OTHER COMPLICATING FACTORS

So how does this affect me and why can't they solve these problems? Well, for starters, the sleep apnea continues to keep the fistulas open. Most of the treatments for the apnea use pressurized systems (C-PAP and BI-PAP machines) to pump air into the body at night. This causes an increase in head pressure, which tends to reopen or keep the fistulas open. As I mentioned in the book, there are several other treatment options, but the only ones applicable to me were sleeping on an incline and taking medications to keep my airway open.

With the apnea problem, it is foolish to attempt another fistula repair. Episodes of apnea subsequent to the repair risk compromising the newly grafted tissue. If the fistulas could be repaired, it is possible that some of the sleep treatments would work. If the sleep apnea could be controlled, the fistulas might repair themselves, or surgery might work a second time. Neither side can fix the ongoing problems I have at this point, so the circle continues.

To make things more complicated, we are still not entirely sure how the brain stem damage affects my situation. Is it causing some of the apnea episodes? The technology is not advanced enough presently to give us answers. Also, add the difficulties sleeping and things get really complex. I sleep very poorly, which makes me more tired and more easily agitated during the day. The vestibular disorders in themselves make everyday life tiring and irritating, so now it's a double whammy. The effort it takes to get through the day leaves me with little or no energy for things such as filtering out noises or keeping myself upright or recalling important data. It also leaves me with little or no reserve to keep my emotions in check. I am easily irritated, sometimes snappy and quick to be teary-eyed. I am using so much energy just to do the daily things people take for granted that by the end of the day I have exhausted all of my resources, and I cannot get enough REM or deep sleep to feel rested to start it all again the next day.

I have been the "test patient" for several medications concerning my sleep apnea and restless leg syndrome. Currently I am taking a medication to keep my airway toned during the night and several medications to try to control my leg jerking. Many of these have a side effect of dizziness, lightheadedness, nausea and a series of other unpleasantries. As I am also taking a medication to control the headaches due to the inner ear problems, one to regulate the fluid flow in the ear and a shot to keep me from menstruating (this has helped tremendously with the fluid and hormonal changes that were causing many symptoms during my period), all of the medications affect each other. Fortunately, I have found a mix of medications that are interacting with each other very well, but it took a long time and a lot of nausea to get there, and all of these drugs are for maintenance and are not a cure.

MY PHYSICAL THERAPY EXPERIENCE

(This is my experience with my personal physical therapist. It is not an endorsement or a "how to" program. Only a licensed therapist can design a program meant for you. Please check with a doctor and therapist before beginning any exercises).

The therapists who specialize in inner-ear disorders are few and far between. My ear doctor referred me to a therapist who had done a lot of research and had a lot of experience with inner-ear patients. It was extremely important to me to have a therapist who knew all of the fistula precautions because physical therapy involves movement and I needed someone who would know what I was not supposed to do, was creative enough to help solve some unique problems, and to answer some difficult questions.

To begin with, she asked what my goals were during therapy because we both knew that therapy would not be a cure for me. My goals were to keep some muscle tone, lose some weight, if possible, and give me some satisfaction by allowing me to do a little moving and stretching. I also wanted to ease some tension in my neck and back and begin to do some exercises to make it easier for me to look around and balance myself.

We began our first session doing some routine vestibular testing for nystagmus (involuntary, coordinated eye movements that occur as the head moves or as the eyes follow a moving object) and balance functions, testing both with my eyes open and closed when possible. We also did a fairly in-depth "interview" concerning my ailments, my experience with physical therapy and my feelings about the therapy. Since I had once been a physical therapy student, I let her know that I wanted to know why she was doing things. My entire medical situation is very interesting to me scientifically. Sometimes I am able to remove myself from the situation enough to look at things scholastically. Other times, I am just a patient with ailments, and it is much more difficult to be fascinated by a disease or injury when you just feel exhausted and miserable and don't have the ability to be objective. Each day of therapy I would tell her which category I felt I was in (removed scientist or tired patient) and we would begin from there.

One of my first tasks was designed to improve my visual tracking. The first exercises were done in a chair because I could not even sit without random movement. The first exercises were called "smooth pursuits." Before we could effectively do these we did several exercises designed to teach my system to use touch more effectively to tell me where I was in relation to the room and ground. I would concentrate on feeling my feet (with socks or bare feet) firmly on the ground. I needed to concentrate on my butt in the seat, my back in the chair and "feeling" where I was. Also, I was to concentrate on breathing in and out in a rhythmic fashion and in a soothing, calming manner. The breathing exercises and feeling my feet on the floor and my butt in the seat, my arms on the arm rests would allow me to re-center myself when I was dizzy or tired or both.

When we began the smooth pursuits, I was seated with my head and eyes forward. I was to hold my thumb of my right hand straight out in front of me, then slowly move it horizontally side to side about six inches in each direction, following the movement with my eyes only. I repeated this three to five times and then would report on how it made me feel (dizzy, as if in slow motion, etc.). I was to work on this until I could do it fairly easily without getting dizzy or feeling nauseated. I would also do a similar exercise, moving my thumb vertically, up and down.

Another exercise we began was saccades. Again,

seated in the same position, I was to hold both thumbs out about six inches apart from each other and then quickly look from one thumb to the other, then rest, re-center and do it again three to five times. The next exercise was holding the thumbs six inches apart vertically and doing the same thing. Once I was able to do that fairly well, I moved my thumbs in toward each other about two inches and repeated the exercises.

We probably worked on just these basic exercises for several months. The easier it got, the more we would add. After a while, we tried these exercises with me sitting away from the back of the chair. This was much more difficult because I had less information to keep me in tune with the surroundings. The next step was to try it standing when I was having a "good" day.

I think we both realized and admitted to each other that this was going to be a very long and slow process because my system was so damaged. Even knowing that, I was amazed at how exhausted I was after only one session of doing smooth pursuits or saccades. Sometimes it was very depressing, but we would reevaluate my condition every few visits so that I could track the progress I was making.

The next exercise was head tilting. I would begin with my head centered (and sitting) and slowly bring my chin to my chest and my eyes to the floor. Then I would look up to the ceiling while moving my head upward. The object was to keep from looking at anything in-between the floor and the ceiling. We began doing this slowly, stopping after each repetition to re-center myself. We progressed to faster movements and also began to do it with my eyes closed and while standing (eyes open). This was an exhausting exercise, so I usually could not do more than five repetitions. I also progressed to doing this exercise with my head turning from left to right, selecting an object (usually a bright sticker we placed on the walls) to focus on.

The next goal was to try some weight shifts. First we had to do more centering exercises while standing. Because there is much less proprioceptive information available while standing, most of the focus involved feeling my feet on the ground, my muscles in my ankles moving to keep myself balanced, the muscles in my legs and hips, and focusing on alignment using a mirror. This was complicated for me because I have scoliosis and my hips and back are uneven. I had adapted to this, but was not standing straight, so I had to relearn how to stand in a more correct alignment.

Once we had practiced alignment and more proprioceptive techniques, I was to do the weight shifts. Standing with my feet approximately the same distance apart as my shoulders, I would concentrate on shifting my weight ever so slightly to my right foot without losing my balance. Then to the center, then to the left. Eventually I tried it with my eyes closed (and my therapist close by to catch me).

This was much harder, but did show the value of the proprioceptive training.

Next we did weight shifts going from center to forward, moving from my ankles and not my hips. We were not able to do weight shifts backward because I would always lose my balance. Backward movement and tilting the head up are probably the hardest movements for vestibular patients because they are so unnatural and usually unnecessary for daily life. Since I rely on my sight, I am looking at where I am going all the time. Backward motion becomes extremely foreign and unnerving, and looking up is a huge motion change for the head and tends to cause dizziness. As we identify our weaknesses, we tend to rule out any high-risk movements such as that and only move in ways that are comfortable for us. Also, there was little reason to try to teach myself to walk backward, so we concentrated on more useful movements.

Once I was fairly comfortable with all these exercises, it was time to try some walking. First, we had to calculate a heart rate that would be ideal for me. Because I was not to exert myself in a way that would cause my blood pressure to rise much (or this would increase my head and chest pressure), we knew that I would have to keep my heart rate well below the "target" heart rate for people exercising, and definitely below the maximum heart rate level for "normal" people. As the general equation for figuring out the target training heart rate is (220-age) x .65 (low-end target rate) and .80 (high-end target rate) = training zone, we did that calculation and decided that my heart rate should definitely not even get in the low-end target training rate. Our maximum heart rate turned out to be about 120 beats per minute.

Keeping this in mind, we started by taking my "resting pulse," and then having me walk on the treadmill at the lowest speed for one minute. We then took my pulse again and recorded it.

The following sessions we would do several of the tracking and balance exercises and then do one minute of walking. This increased to two, then three, then five minutes at a time and ultimately ended with walking ten minutes at a time at 1.1 miles per hour. We actually found that, after several weeks, the walking would decrease my "resting heart rate"!

During some of our sessions, when I was feeling particularly nauseated or unwell, we would work on decreasing the tension in my neck and shoulders. I couldn't lie on a massage table with my head down, so we had to be creative and come up with a way to stack pillows onto the table so I could sit in a chair and just lean forward to relax. She would then do either some acupressure techniques, or at times, some ultrasound on my shoulders. We had to be very careful not to get too close to my neck and head, since ultrasound tends to increase the blood flow to the area. If it gets too warm too quickly, the ears also respond, creating the dizzy symptoms (and tensing up) that we were trying to counteract.

I had mixed feelings about going to therapy. Sometimes it would make me sad because I would think about the things I wasn't going to get to do that I had planned. Other times, I was glad that I had some experience on the therapist's side of the table because it gave me a greater appreciation for what we were doing and a greater understanding of the time and effort it would take to get results. I also understood the importance of doing the therapy at home, although it would often make me sick.

I was glad that I had a therapist who was educated about my particular problems and was honest enough to tell me when she didn't know how to approach something. She was also determined enough to investigate those things further to try to get answers to help me. Ultimately, I think that it definitely did me some good, and has allowed me to feel a bit more active and healthier than before. I have been faithful about doing my walking, and we even worked out a few stretching exercises I could do without bending over or exerting pressure.

I took a break from physical therapy when I started doing some more intense vision therapy. Progressing in one area of therapy is difficult enough without adding another therapy that also requires energy and focus. I have since been on a maintenance plan for both visual and physical therapy. I realized that it is easy to get overloaded with doctor and therapy appointments and daily activities, and I was beginning to have a difficult time doing any therapy at all. I would dread the appointments and the "homework" that went along with them, so I elected to be on a maintenance plan, checking in from time to time if I was having problems or felt particularly motivated to do additional work.

All in all, I have been quite pleased with my therapists and doctors. We have done a lot of work together, knowing that the rewards would come in small increments and in long intervals.

I've found, as I'm sure I would have had I become a physical therapist myself, that patience, persistence and good communication are the keys to success.

Bill and I, soulmates

To order a copy of
Invisible Illnesses and Disabilities...

Please send your name, address, (and e-mail address if you have one), plus:

$14.95 (check or money order)* per book, and
$2.50 shipping and handling (in U.S.)** per book to:

To: W.E. Merritt
P.O. Box 55273
Portland, OR 97238-5273

Number of books wanted_____   x $14.95=_____
Shipping/handling: # of books____   x $ 2.50=_____

Total books ordered:_____
Total enclosed: _____

For more information, e-mail:
Smith-Merritt@worldnet.att.net
or visit our web page: http://home.att.net/~Smith-Merritt

*Cashiers checks and money orders will ensure immediate shipping. Personal checks must clear before book(s) will be shipped.
**For orders shipped outside the U.S. or large quantity orders, please write or e-mail for the postage due.

Lifestyles Press web page: www.lifestylespress.com